SET APART
FOR
SERVICE

NATIONAL CONFERENCE OF CATHOLIC BISHOPS
1312 MASSACHUSETTS AVENUE, N.W.
WASHINGTON, D.C. 20005

OFFICE OF THE PRESIDENT

February 15, 1982

To the Rectors, Faculty and Students of the
American Seminaries:

    At the suggestion of His Eminence William Cardinal Baum of the Sacred Congregation for Catholic Education and with my blessing, the Daughters of Saint Paul, working with the Bishops' Committee on Priestly Formation of the United States Catholic Conference, present to the American seminaries and in particular to our American seminarians this edition of the talks of Pope Paul VI and His Holiness Pope John Paul II to seminaries and seminarians.

    From the beginning of his Pontificate, our present Holy Father has indicated over and over again his special predilection for seminarians and in particular his concern for their proper preparation for the work they will undertake as his co-laborers with Christ in the work of bringing God to the world and the world to God.

    I commend to your reading these talks and allocutions, knowing that you will find herein encouragement for your present work and formation and inspiration for the days ahead.

    Sincerely yours in Christ,

    + *John R. Roach*

    Most Rev. John R. Roach
    Archbishop of Saint Paul and Minneapolis
    President, NCCB/USCC

SET APART FOR SERVICE

By
POPE PAUL VI
and
POPE JOHN PAUL II

Foreword by
WILLIAM CARDINAL BAUM

ST. PAUL EDITIONS

Documents and discourses in this work, unless otherwise indicated, are reprinted with permission of *L'Osservatore Romano*.

ISBN 0-8198-6832-9 cloth
      0-8198-6833-7 paper

Cover Design: Daughters of St. Paul

Copyright © 1982, by the Daughters of St. Paul

Printed in the U.S.A. by the Daughters of St. Paul
50 St. Paul's Ave., Boston, MA 02130

The Daughters of St. Paul are an international congregation of religious women serving the Church with the communications media.

Contents

Foreword 11

POPE PAUL VI

Priestly Celibacy 15
Encyclical Letter of June 24, 1967

POPE JOHN PAUL II

To All Bishops of the Church 73
On the occasion of Holy Thursday, 1979

To All the Priests of the Church 79
On the occasion of Holy Thursday, 1979

Great Promise for the Future
of Evangelization 109
To priests, religious and seminarians of the archdiocese of Philadelphia, Pennsylvania, on October 3, 1979

A Deep Commitment to Authentic
Christian Living 117
To professors and theologians of the Catholic University of America, on October 7, 1979

Theology Dynamically Involved in the
Prophetic Mission of the Church 125
Address at the Pontifical Gregorian University, on December 15, 1979

Your Lives Offer Promise
for the Church's Future 143
Homily at Mass celebrated at the Pontifical North American College, Rome, Italy, on February 22, 1980

On the Mystery and Worship
of the Eucharist 149
> *Letter to all bishops of the Church,
> February 24, 1980*

Generously Available for the Church's
Needs 197
> *To seminarians and priests at Issy les
> Moulineaux, France, June 1, 1980*

Meet the New Realities of Seminaries
Responsibly 203
> *Address to rectors, spiritual directors and
> prefects of studies of all the major seminaries of Italy, on January 5, 1982*

"Do Whatever He Tells You!" 213
> *Homily at Mass celebrated at the Pontifical Philippine College in Rome, Italy,
> on January 30, 1982*

Foreword

The changes and transformation which have marked the life of our society and of the Church in recent years have also notably influenced our centers of priestly formation. In taking praiseworthy initiatives aimed at renewing our approach to priestly formation in ways better suited to the needs of our time, our seminaries have also witnessed attempts at research and experimentation which call for analysis in the light of the teaching of the Second Vatican Council and of the directives of the Holy See.

In view of this situation and of the ever-increasing demands made upon our seminaries, the stimulus and guidance of the ecclesiastical Magisterium remains a necessity in order to insure a sound preparation of candidates for the priesthood.

The documents published in this volume through the admirable initiative of the Bishops' Committee on Priestly Formation of the National Conference of Catholic Bishops of the United States of America are indeed the expression of the great love and thoughtful solicitude of the Church for her future priests. The substance of these documents, as well as the goals they set forth and the directives they include, present an educational ideal particularly appropriate to guarantee an integrated priestly formation under its different aspects: human maturity, spiritual growth, and intellectual and apostolic preparation.

It is my hope that this volume will find wide acceptance, and be read with appreciation, in all centers of priestly formation. A careful study of the documents contained in this volume will significantly help to develop and strengthen the vitality of our seminaries in accordance with the often expressed hopes of our Holy Father, Pope John Paul II.

Rome, January 29, 1982

✠ WILLIAM CARDINAL BAUM,
*Prefect of the Sacred Congregation
for Catholic Education*

POPE PAUL VI

Priestly Celibacy

Sacerdotalis Caelibatus

Encyclical Letter of June 24, 1967*

Consecrated Celibacy Today

1. Priestly celibacy has been guarded by the Church for centuries as a brilliant jewel, and retains its value undiminished even in our time when mentality and structures have undergone such profound change.

Amid the modern stirrings of opinion, a tendency has also been manifested, and even a desire expressed, to ask the Church to re-examine this characteristic institution of hers. It is said that in the world of our time its observance has come to be of doubtful value and almost impossible.

A Promise We Made

2. This state of affairs is troubling consciences, perplexing some priests and young aspirants to the priesthood; it is a cause for alarm

---

*N.C.W.C. translation.

in many of the faithful and constrains us to fulfill the promise we made to the Council Fathers. We told them that it was our intention to give new luster and strength to priestly celibacy in the world of today.[1] Since saying this we have over a considerable period of time earnestly implored the enlightenment and assistance of the Holy Spirit and have examined before God opinions and petitions which have come to us from all over the world, notably from some pastors of God's Church.

Breadth and Gravity of the Question

3. The great question concerning the sacred celibacy of the clergy in the Church has long been before our mind in its deep seriousness: must that grave, ennobling obligation remain today for those who have the intention of receiving major orders? Is it possible or appropriate nowadays to observe such an obligation? Has the time not come to break the bond linking celibacy with the priesthood in the Church? Could the difficult observance of it not be made optional? Would this not be a way to help the priestly ministry and facilitate ecumenical approaches? And if the golden law of sacred celibacy is to remain, what reasons are there to show that it is holy and fitting? What means are to be taken to observe it, and how can it be changed from a burden to a help for the priestly life?

Facts and Problems

4. Our attention has rested particularly on the objections which have been and are still

made in various forms against the retention of sacred celibacy. In virtue of our apostolic office we are obliged by the importance, and indeed complexity, of the subject to give faithful consideration to the facts and the problems they involve, at the same time bringing to them, as it is our duty and our mission to do, the light of truth which is Christ. Our intention is to do in all things the will of Him who has called us to this office and to show what we are in the Church, the servant of God's servants.

OBJECTIONS AGAINST PRIESTLY CELIBACY

Celibacy and the New Testament

5. It may be said that today ecclesiastical celibacy has been examined more penetratingly than ever before and in all its aspects. It has been examined from the doctrinal, historical, sociological, psychological and pastoral point of view. The intentions prompting this examination have frequently been basically correct although reports may sometimes have distorted them.

Let us look openly at the principal objections against the law that links ecclesiastical celibacy with the priesthood.

The first seems to come from the most authoritative source, the New Testament, which preserves the teaching of Christ and the Apostles. It does not demand celibacy of sacred ministers but proposes it rather as a free act of obedience to a special vocation or to a special spiritual gift (cf. Mt. 19:11-12). Jesus Himself did not make it a prerequisite in His choice of the Twelve, nor did the Apostles for those who presided over the first Christian communities (cf. 1 Tm. 3:2-5; Ti. 1:5-6).

The Fathers of the Church

6. The close relationship that the Fathers of the Church and ecclesiastical writers made over the centuries between the ministering priesthood and celibacy has its origin in a mentality and historical situations far different from ours. In patristic texts more frequently we find exhortations to the clergy to abstain from marital relations rather than those which recommend that they observe celibacy; and the reasons justifying the perfect chastity of the Church's ministers seem often to be based on an over-pessimistic view of man's earthly condition or on a certain notion of the purity necessary for contact with sacred things. In addition, it is said that the old arguments no longer are in harmony with the different social and cultural milieus in which the Church today, through her priests, is called upon to work.

Vocation and Celibacy

7. Many see a difficulty in the fact that in the present discipline concerning celibacy the gift of a vocation to the priesthood is identified with that of perfect chastity as a state of life for God's ministers. And so people ask whether it be right to exclude from the priesthood those who, it is claimed, have been called to the ministry without having been called to lead a celibate life.

Celibacy and Shortage of Priests

8. It is asserted, moreover, that the maintaining of priestly celibacy in the Church does great harm in those regions where the shortage of the clergy—a fact recognized with sadness and deplored by the same Council[2]—gives rise to critical situations; that it prevents the full realization of the divine plan of salvation and at times jeopardizes the very possibility of the initial proclamation of the Gospel. Thus the disquieting decline in the ranks of the clergy is attributed by some to the heavy burden of the obligation of celibacy.

Difficulties of Celibacy

9. Then there are those who are convinced that a married priesthood would remove the occasions for infidelity, waywardness and distressing defections which hurt and sadden the whole Church. These also maintain that a married priesthood would enable Christ's ministers to witness more fully to Christian living, by including the witness of married life, from which they are excluded by their state of life.

Violence to Nature?

10. There are also some who strongly maintain that priests by reason of their celibacy find themselves in a situation that is physically and psychologically detrimental to the development of a mature and well-balanced human personality. And so it happens, they say, that priests often become hard and lacking in human warmth; that, excluded from sharing fully the

life and destiny of the rest of their brothers, they are obliged to live a life of solitude which leads to bitterness and discouragement.

Is all this perhaps indicative of unwarranted violence to nature and an unjustified disparagement of human values which have their source in the divine work of creation and have been made whole through the work of the redemption accomplished by Christ?

Inadequate Formation

11. Again, in view of the way in which a candidate for the priesthood comes to accept an obligation as momentous as this, the objection is raised that in practice this acceptance results, not from an authentically personal decision, but rather from an attitude of passivity, the fruit of a formation that is neither adequate nor one that makes sufficient allowance for human liberty. For the degree of knowledge and power of decision of a young person and his psychological and physical maturity fall far below—or at any rate are disproportionate to—the seriousness of the obligation he is assuming, its real difficulties and its permanence.

Correct Points of View

12. We well realize that there are other objections that can be made against priestly celibacy. It is a very complex question and one which touches intimately on the ordinary view of life, to which it brings the shining light of divine revelation. A never-ending series of difficulties

will present themselves to those who "cannot receive this precept" (Mt. 19:11), and who do not know or who forget the "gift of God" (cf. Jn. 4:10), and who are unaware of the higher logic of that new concept of life, its wonderful efficacy and abundant riches.

Testimony of the Past and Present

13. The sum of these objections would appear to drown out the solemn and age-old voice of the pastors of the Church and of the masters of the spiritual life and to nullify the living testimony of the countless ranks of saints and faithful ministers of God, for whom celibacy has been the object of the total and generous gift of themselves to the mystery of Christ, as well as its outward sign. But no, this voice, still strong and untroubled, is the voice not just of the past but of the present too. Ever intent on seeing things as they are, we cannot close our eyes to this magnificent, wonderful reality: that there are still today in God's holy Church, in every part of the world where she exercises her beneficent influence, great numbers of her ministers—subdeacons, deacons, priests and bishops—who are living their life of voluntary and consecrated celibacy in the most exemplary way. Nor can we overlook the immense ranks of religious men and women at their side, of laity and of young people too, united in the faithful observance of perfect chastity. They live in chastity, not out of disdain for the gift of life, but because of a greater love for that new life which springs from the Paschal

Mystery. They live this life of courageous self-denial and spiritual joyfulness with exemplary fidelity and also with relative facility. This magnificent phenomenon bears testimony to an exceptional facet of the kingdom of God living in the midst of modern society, to which it renders humble and beneficial service as the "light of the world" and the "salt of the earth" (cf. Mt. 5:13-14). We cannot withhold the expression of our admiration; the spirit of Christ is certainly breathing here.

Validity of Celibacy Confirmed

14. Hence we consider that the present law of celibacy should today continue to be firmly linked to the ecclesiastical ministry. This law should support the minister in his exclusive, definitive and total choice of the unique and supreme love of Christ; it should uphold him in the entire dedication of himself to the public worship of God and to the service of the Church; it should characterize his state of life both among the faithful and in the world at large.

Power of the Church

15. The gift of the priestly vocation dedicated to the divine worship and to the religious and pastoral service of the People of God is undoubtedly distinct from that which leads a person to choose celibacy as a state of consecrated life (cf. #5, 7). But the priestly vocation, although inspired by God, does not become

definitive or operative without having been tested and accepted by those in the Church who hold power and bear responsibility for the ministry serving the ecclesial community. It is therefore the task of those who hold authority in the Church to determine in accordance with the varying conditions of time and place, who in actual practice are to be considered suitable candidates for the religious and pastoral service of the Church, and what should be required of them.

Purpose of the Encyclical

16. In a spirit of faith, therefore, we look on this occasion afforded us by Divine Providence as a favorable opportunity for setting forth anew and in a way more suited to the men of our time, the fundamental reasons for sacred celibacy. If difficulties against faith "can stimulate the mind to a more accurate and penetrating grasp" of it,[3] the same is true of the ecclesiastical discipline which guides and directs the life of the faithful.

We are deeply moved by the joy this occasion gives us of contemplating this aspect of the divine riches and beauty of the Church of Christ. Her beauty may not always be immediately apparent to the human eye, because it is the fruit of the love of the divine Head of the Church and because it reveals itself in that perfection of holiness (cf. Eph. 5:25-27) which moves the human spirit to admiration, since it finds the resources of the human creature inadequate to account for it.

FIRST PART

I. Reasons for Sacred Celibacy

The Council and Celibacy

17. Virginity undoubtedly, as the Second Vatican Council declared, "is not, indeed, demanded by the very nature of the priesthood, as is evident from the practice of the primitive Church and from the tradition of the Eastern Churches."[4] But at the same time the Council did not hesitate to confirm solemnly the ancient, sacred and providential present law of priestly celibacy. In addition, it set forth the motives which justify this law for those who, in a spirit of faith and with generous fervor, know how to appreciate the gifts of God.

New Light on Old Arguments

18. Consideration of the "manifold suitability" *(loc. cit.)* of celibacy for God's ministers is not something recent. Even if the explicit reasons have differed with different mentalities and different situations, they were always inspired by specifically Christian considerations; and from these considerations we can get an intuition of the more fundamental motives underlying them. These can be brought into greater evidence only under the influence of the Holy Spirit, promised by Christ to His followers for the knowledge of things to come (cf. Jn. 16:13) and to enable the

People of God to increase in the understanding of the mystery of Christ and of the Church. In this process the experience gained through the ages from a deeper penetration of spiritual things also has its part.[5]

THE CHRISTOLOGICAL SIGNIFICANCE OF CELIBACY

The Newness of Christ

19. The Christian priesthood, being of a new order, can be understood only in the light of the newness of Christ, the Supreme Pontiff and eternal Priest, who instituted the priesthood of the ministry as a real participation in His own unique priesthood.[6] The minister of Christ and dispenser of the mysteries of God (1 Cor. 4:1), therefore, looks up to Him directly as his model and supreme ideal (cf. 1 Cor. 11:1). The Lord Jesus, the only Son of God, was sent by the Father into the world, and He became man, in order that humanity which was subject to sin and death might be reborn, and through this new birth (Jn. 3:5; Ti. 3:5) might enter the kingdom of heaven. Being entirely consecrated to the will of the Father (Jn. 4:34; 17:4), Jesus brought forth this new creation by means of His Paschal Mystery (2 Cor. 5:17; Gal. 6:15); thus, He introduced into time and into the world a new form of life which is sublime and divine and which transforms the very earthly condition of human nature (cf. Gal. 3:28).

Matrimony and Celibacy in the Newness of Christ

20. Matrimony according to the will of God continues the work of the first creation (Gn. 2:18); and considered within the total plan of salvation, it even acquires a new meaning and a new value. Jesus, in fact, has restored its original dignity (Mt. 19:3-8), has honored it (Jn. 2:1-11) and has raised it to the dignity of a sacrament and of a mysterious symbol of His own union with the Church (Eph. 5:32). Thus, Christian couples walk together toward their heavenly fatherland in the exercise of mutual love, in the fulfillment of their particular obligations, and in striving for the sanctity proper to them. But Christ, Mediator of a more excellent Testament (Heb. 8:6), has also opened a new way, in which the human creature adheres wholly and directly to the Lord, and is concerned only with Him and with His affairs (1 Cor. 7:33-35); thus, he manifests in a clearer and more complete way the profoundly transforming reality of the New Testament.

Celibacy and Priesthood in Christ the Mediator

21. Christ, the only Son of the Father, by the power of the Incarnation itself was made Mediator between heaven and earth, between the Father and the human race. Wholly in accord with this mission, Christ remained throughout His whole life in the state of celibacy, which signified His total dedication to the service of God and men. This deep connection between celibacy and the priesthood of Christ is reflected in those

whose fortune it is to share in the dignity and in the mission of the Mediator and eternal Priest; this sharing will be more perfect the freer the sacred minister is from the bonds of flesh and blood.[7]

Celibacy for the Kingdom of Heaven

22. Jesus, who selected the first ministers of salvation, wished them to be introduced to the understanding of the mysteries of the kingdom of heaven (Mt. 13:11; Mk. 4:11; Lk. 8:10), to be co-workers with God under a very special title, and His ambassadors (2 Cor. 5:20). He called them friends and brethren (Jn. 15:15; 20:17), for whom He consecrated Himself so that they might be consecrated in truth (Jn. 17:19), He promised a more than abundant recompense to anyone who should leave home, family, wife and children for the sake of the kingdom of God (Lk. 18:29-30). More than this, in words filled with mystery and hope, He also commended[8] an even more perfect consecration to the kingdom of heaven by means of celibacy, as a special gift (Mt. 19:11-12). The motive of this answer to the divine call is the kingdom of heaven *(ibid.,* v. 12); similarly, the ideas—of this kingdom (Lk. 18:30), of the Gospel (Mk. 10:29), and of the name of Christ (Mt. 19:29), are what motivate those invited by Jesus to the difficult renunciations of the apostolate, by a very intimate participation in His lot (cf. Mk., *loc. cit.).*

Testimony to Christ

23. This, then, is the mystery of the newness of Christ, of all that He is and stands for; it is

the sum of the highest ideals of the Gospel and of the kingdom; it is a particular manifestation of grace, which springs from the Paschal Mystery of the Savior and renders the choice of celibacy desirable and worthwhile on the part of those called by our Lord Jesus. Thus, they intend not only to participate in Christ's priestly office, but also to share with Him His very condition of living.

Fullness of Love

24. The response to the divine call is an answer of love to the love which Christ has shown us so sublimely (Jn. 15:13; 3:16). This response is included in the mystery of that special love for those souls who have accepted His most urgent appeals (cf. Mk. 10:21). Grace with a divine force increases the longings of love. And love, when it is genuine, is total, exclusive, stable and lasting, an irresistible spur to all forms of heroism. And so, the free choice of sacred celibacy has always been considered by the Church "as something that signifies and stimulates charity"[9]; it signifies a love without reservations, it stimulates to a charity which is open to all. Who can see in such a life, so completely dedicated and motivated as shown above, the sign of a spiritual poverty, of self-seeking, and not rather see that celibacy is and ought to be a rare and very meaningful example of a life whose motivation is love, by which man expresses his own unique greatness? Who can doubt the moral and spiritual richness of such a consecrated life, consecrated not to any human ideal no matter

how noble, but to Christ and to His work to bring about a new form of humanity in all places and for all generations?

Invitation to Study

25. This biblical and theological vision associates our ministerial priesthood with the priesthood of Christ; it is modeled on the total and exclusive dedication of Christ to His mission of salvation, and makes it the cause of our assimilation to the form of charity and sacrifice proper to Christ our Savior. This vision seems to us so profound and rich in truth, both speculative and practical, that we invite you, venerable brothers, and we invite you, eager students of Christian doctrine and masters of the spiritual life, and all priests who have gained a supernatural insight into your vocation—to persevere in the study of this vision, and to go deeply into the inner recesses and wealth of its reality. In this way, the bond between the priesthood and celibacy will be seen in an ever improving union, owing to its clear logic and to the heroism of a unique and limitless love for Christ the Lord and for His Church.

THE ECCLESIOLOGICAL SIGNIFICANCE OF CELIBACY

Celibacy and the Love of Christ and of the Priest for the Church

26. "Made captive by Christ Jesus" (Phil. 3:12) unto the complete abandonment of one's

entire self to Him, the priest takes on the likeness of Christ most perfectly, even in the love with which the eternal Priest has loved the Church, His Body, and offered Himself entirely for her sake, in order to make her a glorious, holy and immaculate Spouse (cf. Eph. 5:25-27).

The consecrated celibacy of the sacred ministers actually manifests the virginal love of Christ for the Church, and the virginal and supernatural fecundity of this marriage, by which the children of God are born but not of flesh and blood (Jn. 1:13).[10]

Unity and Harmony of the Priest's Life: the Ministry of the Word

27. The priest dedicates himself to the service of the Lord Jesus and of His Mystical Body with complete liberty, which is made easier by his total offering, and he realizes more fully the unity and harmony of the priestly life.[11] His ability increases for listening to the Word of God and for prayer. Indeed, the Word of God, as preserved by the Church, stirs up in the priest, who daily meditates on it, lives it and preaches it to the faithful, echoes that are vibrant and profound.

Divine Office and Prayer

28. Like Christ Himself, His minister is wholly and solely intent on the things of God and the Church (cf. Lk. 2:49; 1 Cor. 7:32-33), and he imitates the great high Priest who stands in the presence of God ever living to intercede in our favor (Heb. 9:24; 7:25). So, he receives joy and encouragement unceasingly from the attentive

and devout recitation of the Divine Office, by which he dedicates his voice to the Church who prays together with her Spouse,[12] and he recognizes the necessity of continuing his diligence at prayer, which is the profoundly priestly occupation (Acts 6:4).

The Ministry of Grace and of the Eucharist

29. The rest of a priest's life acquires a greater richness of meaning and sanctifying power. In fact, his individual efforts at his own sanctification find new incentives in the ministry of grace and in the ministry of the Eucharist, in which all the riches of the Church are contained[13]: acting in the person of Christ, the priest unites himself most intimately with the offering, and places on the altar his entire life, which bears the marks of the holocaust.

A Life Most Full and Fruitful

30. What other considerations can we make to describe the increase of the priest's power, of his service, his love and his sacrifice for the entire People of God? Christ spoke of Himself: "Unless a grain of wheat falls into the earth and dies, it remains alone; but if it dies, it bears much fruit" (Jn. 12:24). And the Apostle Paul did not hesitate to expose himself to a daily death, in order to obtain among his faithful glory in Christ Jesus (1 Cor. 15:31). In a similar way, by a daily dying to himself, and by giving up the legitimate love of a family of his own for the love of Christ and of His kingdom, the priest will find the glory of an

exceedingly rich and fruitful life in Christ, because like Him and in Him, he loves and dedicates himself to all the children of God.

The Celibate Priest in the Community of the Faithful

31. In the community of the faithful committed to his charge, the priest is Christ present. Thus, it is most fitting that in all things he should reproduce the image of Christ and follow in particular His example, both in his personal as well as in his apostolic life. To his children in Christ, the priest is a sign and a pledge of that sublime and new reality which is the kingdom of God, of which he is the dispenser; he possesses it on his own account and to a more perfect degree, and nourishes the faith and the hope of all Christians, who because they are such, are bound to observe chastity according to their proper state of life.

The Pastoral Efficacy of Celibacy

32. The consecration to Christ, by virtue of a new and lofty title like celibacy, evidently gives to the priest, even in the practical field, the maximum efficiency and the best disposition of mind, psychologically and affectively, for the continuous exercise of a perfect charity. This charity will permit him to spend himself wholly for the welfare of all, in a fuller and more concrete way (2 Cor. 12:15).[14] It also guarantees him obviously a greater freedom and flexibility in the pastoral ministry,[15] in his active and loving presence in the world, to which Christ has invited him (Jn.

17:18), so that he may pay fully to all the children of God the debt due them (Rom. 1:14).

THE ESCHATOLOGICAL SIGNIFICANCE OF CELIBACY

The Longing of the People of God for the Heavenly Kingdom

33. The kingdom of God which is not of this world (Jn. 18:36) is present here on earth in mystery, and will reach her perfection with the glorious coming of the Lord Jesus.[16] The Church here below constitutes the seed and the beginning of this kingdom. And as she continues to grow slowly but surely, she longs for the perfect kingdom and desires vehemently with all her energy to unite herself with her King in glory.[17]

The pilgrim People of God, as seen in history, is on a journey toward its true homeland (Phil. 3:20), where the divine sonship of the redeemed (1 Jn. 3:2) will be fully revealed and where its splendor will be definitively attained by the transformed loveliness of the Spouse of the Lamb of God.[18]

Celibacy as a Sign of Heavenly Treasures

34. Our Lord and Master has said that "in the resurrection they neither marry nor are given in marriage, but are like angels in heaven" (Mt. 22:30). In the world of man, so deeply involved in earthly concerns and too often enslaved by the desires of the flesh (cf. 1 Jn. 2:16), the precious divine gift of perfect continence for the kingdom

of heaven stands out precisely as "a singular sign of the blessings of heaven,"[19] it proclaims the presence on earth of the final stages of salvation (cf. 1 Cor. 7:29-31) with the arrival of a new world, and in a way it anticipates the fulfillment of the kingdom as it sets forth its supreme values which will one day shine forth in all the children of God. This continence, therefore, stands as a testimony to the necessary progress of the People of God toward the final goal of their earthly pilgrimage, and as a stimulus for all to raise their eyes to the things above, where Christ sits at the right hand of the Father and where our life is hidden in Christ with God until He appears in glory (Col. 3:1-4).

II. Celibacy in the Life of the Church

Antiquity

35. Although it would be too long, still it would be quite instructive to study the historical documents on ecclesiastical celibacy. Let the following indication suffice. In Christian antiquity the Fathers and ecclesiastical writers testify to the spread through the East and the West of the voluntary practice of celibacy by sacred ministers[20] because of its profound suitability for their total dedication to the service of Christ and of His Church.

The Church of the West

36. The Church of the West, from the beginning of the fourth century, strengthened, spread,

and approved this practice by means of various provincial councils and through the Supreme Pontiffs.[21] More than any others, the supreme Pastors and teachers of the Church of God, the guardians and interpreters of the patrimony of the faith and of holy Christian practices, promoted, defended, and restored ecclesiastical celibacy in successive eras of history, even when they met opposition from the clergy itself and when the practices of a decadent society did not favor the heroic demands of virtue. The obligation of celibacy was then solemnly sanctioned by the Sacred Ecumenical Council of Trent[22] and finally included in the Code of Canon Law (can. 132 #1).

The Most Recent Papal Teaching

37. The most recent Sovereign Pontiffs who preceded us, making use of their doctrinal knowledge, and spurred on by ardent zeal, strove to enlighten the clergy on this matter, and to urge them to its observance.[23] And we do not wish to fail to pay homage to their revered memory, especially to that of our well-beloved immediate Predecessor which is still fresh in the hearts of men all over the world. During the Roman Synod, with the sincere approval of all the clergy of the city, he spoke as follows: "It deeply hurts us that...anyone can dream that the Church will deliberately or even suitably renounce what from time immemorial has been and still remains, one of the purest and noblest glories of her priesthood. The law of ecclesiastical celibacy and the efforts necessary to preserve it always recall to

mind the struggles of the heroic times when the Church of Christ had to fight for and succeeded in obtaining her threefold glory, always an emblem of victory, that is, the Church of Christ, free, chaste and catholic."[24]

The Church of the East

38. If the legislation of the Eastern Church is different in the matter of discipline with regard to clerical celibacy, as was finally established by the Council in Trullo held in the year 692,[25] and which has been clearly recognized by the Second Vatican Council,[26] this is due to the different historical background of that most noble part of the Church, a situation which the Holy Spirit has providentially and supernaturally influenced.

We ourselves take this opportunity to express our esteem and our respect for all the clergy of the Oriental Churches, and to recognize in them examples of fidelity and zeal which make them worthy of sincere veneration.

The Voice of the Oriental Fathers

39. We find further comforting reasons for continuing to adhere to the observance of the discipline of clerical celibacy in the exaltation of virginity by the Oriental Fathers. We hear within us, for example, the voice of St. Gregory of Nyssa, reminding us that, "the life of virginity is the image of the blessedness that awaits us in the life to come."[27] We are no less assured by the treatment of the priesthood by St. John Chrysostom,

which is still a fruitful subject for reflection. Intent on throwing light on the harmony which must exist between the private life of him who ministers at the altar and the dignity of the order to which his sacred duties belong, he affirmed, "...it is becoming that he who accepts the priesthood be as pure as if he were in heaven."[28]

Significant Signs in Eastern Tradition

40. Further, it is by no means futile to observe that in the East only celibate priests are ordained bishops, and the priests themselves cannot contract marriage after their ordination to the priesthood. This indicates that these venerable Churches also possess to a certain extent the principle of a celibate priesthood. It shows too that there is a certain appropriateness for the Christian priesthood, of which the bishops possess the summit and the fullness, of the observance of celibacy.[29]

The Faithfulness of the Church of the West to Her Own Tradition

41. In any case, the Church of the West cannot weaken her faithful observance of her own tradition. And it is unthinkable that for centuries she has followed a path which, instead of favoring the spiritual richness of individual souls and of the People of God, has in some way compromised it, or that she has with arbitrary juridical prescriptions stifled the free expansion of the most profound realities of nature and of grace.

Particular Cases

42. In virtue of the fundamental norm of the government of the Catholic Church, to which we alluded above (#15), while, on the one hand, the law requiring a freely chosen and perpetual celibacy of those who are admitted to Holy Orders remains unchanged, on the other hand, a study may be allowed of the particular circumstances of married sacred ministers of Churches or other Christian communities separated from the Catholic communion, and of the possibility of admitting to priestly functions those who desire to adhere to the fullness of this communion and to continue to exercise the sacred ministry. The circumstances must be such, however, as not to prejudice the existing discipline regarding the celibacy.

And that the authority of the Church may not hesitate to exercise her power in this matter can be seen from the recent Ecumenical Council which foresaw the possibility of conferring holy diaconate on men of mature age who are already married.[30]

Confirmation

43. All this, however, does not signify a relaxation of the existing law, and must not be interpreted as a prelude to its abolition. There are better things to do besides promoting this hypothesis, which tears down that vigor and love in which celibacy finds security and happiness, and which obscures the true doctrine that justifies its existence and exalts its splendor.

It would be much better to promote serious studies in defense of the spiritual meaning and moral value of virginity and celibacy.[31]

Confidence of the Church

44. Holy virginity is a very special gift. Nevertheless, the whole present-day Church, solemnly and universally represented by the pastors responsible for her welfare (with due respect, as we have said, for the discipline of the Eastern Churches) manifested her absolute faith in the Spirit "that the gift of celibacy, so helpful for the priesthood of the New Testament, will be liberally granted by the Father, on condition that those who participate in Christ's priesthood through the sacrament of Orders, and indeed the whole Church, humbly and perseveringly ask for it."[32]

The Prayer of the People of God

45. We wholeheartedly call on the entire People of God to do their duty in bringing about an increase in priestly vocations.[33] We ask them fervently to beg the Father of all, the divine Spouse of the Church, and the Holy Spirit, her principle of life, through the intercession of the Blessed Virgin Mary, Mother of Christ and of His Church, to pour out, especially at present, this divine gift, which the Father certainly does not wish to give stintingly. They should also fervently pray, in like manner, that souls may dispose themselves to receive it by a profound faith and a generous love. In this way, in our world, which needs God's glory (cf. Rom. 3:23), priests,

ever more perfectly conformed to the one and supreme Priest will be a real glory to Christ (2 Cor. 8:23), and, through them, "the glory of the grace" of God will be magnified in the world of today (cf. Eph. 1:6).

The World of Today and Consecrated Celibacy

46. Yes, venerable and well-beloved brothers in the priesthood, whom we cherish "with the affection of Christ Jesus" (Phil. 1:8), it is truly this world in which we live, tormented by the pains of growth and change, justly proud of its human values and human conquests, which urgently needs the witness of lives consecrated to the highest and most sacred spiritual values. This witness is necessary in order that the refined and incomparable light, radiating from the most sublime virtues of the spirit, may not be wanting to our times.

The Numerical Scarcity of Priests

47. Our Lord Jesus Christ did not hesitate to confide the formidable task of evangelizing the world, as it was then known, to a handful of men to all appearances lacking in number and quality. He bade this "little flock" not to lose heart (Lk. 12:32), for, thanks to His constant assistance (Mt. 28:20), through Him and with Him, they would overcome the world (Jn. 16:33). Jesus has taught us also that the kingdom of God has an intrinsic and unobservable dynamism which enables it to grow without man's awareness of it (Mk. 4:26-29). The harvest of God's kingdom is

great, but the laborers, as in the beginning, are few. Actually, they have never been as numerous as human standards would have judged sufficient. But the Lord of the kingdom demands prayers, that it may be He, the Lord of the harvest, who will send out laborers into His harvest (Mt. 9:37-38). The counsels and prudence of man cannot supersede the hidden wisdom of Him who, in the history of salvation, has challenged man's wisdom and power by His own foolishness and weakness (1 Cor. 1:20-31).

The Courage of Faith

48. We appeal to the courage of faith to express the Church's deepest conviction that a more energetic and generous answer to grace, a more explicit and substantiated hope, a more complete and open witness to the mystery of Christ, will never be the cause of her failing in her salvific mission to all mankind. It is necessary for us to learn to do all things in Him who alone gives strength to souls (Phil. 4:13) and increase to His Church (1 Cor. 3:6-7).

The Root of the Problem

49. It is simply not possible to believe that the abolition of ecclesiastical celibacy would considerably increase the number of priestly vocations: the contemporary experience of those Churches and ecclesial communities which allow their ministers to marry seems to prove the contrary. The cause of the decrease in vocations to the priesthood is to be found elsewhere, especially for example, in the fact that individuals

and families have lost their sense of God and of all that is holy, their esteem for the Church as the institution of salvation through faith and sacraments, the institution which must study the true roots of the problem.

III. Celibacy and Human Values

Celibacy and Love

50. As we said above (cf. #10), the Church is not unaware that the choice of consecrated celibacy, since it involves a series of hard renunciations which affect the very depths of a man, presents also grave difficulties and problems to which the men of today are particularly sensitive. In fact, it might seem that celibacy conflicts with the solemn recognition of human values by the Church in the recent Council. And yet a more careful consideration reveals that the sacrifice of human love as experienced in a family and as offered by the priest for the love of Christ, is really a singular tribute paid to that superior love. Indeed, it is universally recognized that man has always offered to God what is worthy of both the giver and the receiver.

Grace and Nature

51. On the other hand, the Church cannot and should not set aside the fact that the choice of celibacy—provided that it is made with human and Christian prudence and responsibility—is

governed by grace which, far from destroying or doing violence to nature, elevates it and imparts to it supernatural powers and vigor. God, who has created and redeemed man, knows what He can ask of him and gives him everything necessary to be able to do what his Creator and Redeemer asks of him. St. Augustine, who had fully and painfully experienced in himself the nature of man, exclaimed: "Grant what You command, and command what You will."[34]

The Real Weight of the Difficulties

52. A true knowledge of the real difficulties of celibacy is very useful, even necessary, for the priest, so that he may be fully aware of what his celibacy requires to be genuine and beneficial. But with equal fidelity to the truth, these difficulties must not be given greater value or weight than they actually have in the human or religious sphere, or declared impossible of solution.

Celibacy Is Not Contrary to Nature

53. After what science has now ascertained, it is not just to continue repeating (cf. #10) that celibacy is against nature because it runs counter to lawful physical, psychological and affective needs or to claim that a completely mature human personality demands fulfillment of these needs. Man, created to God's image and likeness (Gn. 1:26-27), is not just flesh and blood; the sexual instinct is not all that he has; man is also, and preeminently, understanding, choice, freedom, and thanks to these powers he is, and must

remain, superior to the rest of creation; they give him mastery over his physical, psychological and affective appetites.

The Deep Reason for Celibacy

54. The true, deep reason for dedicated celibacy is, as we have said, the choice of a closer and more complete relationship with the mystery of Christ and the Church for the good of all mankind: in this choice there is no doubt that those highest human values are able to find their fullest expression.

Celibacy as an Exultation of Man

55. The choice of celibacy does not connote ignorance, or the despisal of the sexual instinct and affectivity. That would certainly do damage to the physical and psychological balance. On the contrary it demands clear understanding, careful self-control and a wise sublimation of the psychological life on a higher plane. In this way celibacy sets the whole man on a higher level and makes an effective contribution to his own perfection.

Celibacy and the Development of Personality

56. The natural and lawful desire a man has to love a woman and to raise a family are renounced by celibacy, but marriage and the family are not said to be the only way for fully developing the human person. In the priest's heart, love is by no means extinct. His charity is

drawn from the purest source (cf. 1 Jn. 4:8-16), practiced in the imitation of God and Christ, and no less than any other genuine love is demanding and real (cf. 1 Jn. 3:16-18). It gives the priest a limitless horizon, deepens and gives breadth to his sense of responsibility—a sign of mature personality—and inculcates in him as a sign of a higher and greater fatherhood, a generosity and refinement of heart[35] which offer a superlative enrichment.

Consecrated Celibacy and Marriage

57. All of God's People must give testimony to the mystery of Christ and His kingdom but this witnessing does not take the same form for all. The Church leaves to her married children the function of giving the necessary testimony of a genuinely and fully Christian married and family life. She entrusts to her priests the testimony of a life wholly dedicated to the ever new, absorbing realities of God's kingdom.

If this means that the priest is without a direct personal experience of married life, he will by his training, his ministry and the grace of his office, certainly not lack in knowledge, perhaps a deeper knowledge, of the human heart. This will allow him to meet those problems at their source and give solid support by his advice and assistance to married persons and Christian families (cf. 1 Cor. 2:15). The presence in the Christian family of the priest who is living his life of celibacy to the full will underscore the spiritual dimension of every love worthy of the name, and his personal sacrifice will merit for the faithful united in the holy bond of matrimony the grace of a true union.

The Solitude of the Celibate Priest

58. The priest by reason of his celibacy is a solitary: that is true, but his solitude is not emptiness because it is filled with God and the brimming riches of His kingdom. Moreover, for this solitude, which should be an internal and external plenitude of charity, he has prepared himself, if he has chosen it with full understanding, and not through any proud desire to be different from the rest of men, or to withdraw himself from common responsibilities, or to alienate himself from his brothers, or to show contempt for the world. Though set apart from the world, the priest is not separated from the People of God, because he has been appointed to act on behalf of men (Heb. 5:1), since he is consecrated completely to charity (cf. 1 Cor. 14:4ff.) and to the work for which the Lord has chosen him.[36]

Christ and the Loneliness of the Priest

59. At times loneliness will weigh heavily on the priest, but not for that reason will he regret having generously chosen it. Christ, too, in the most tragic hours of His life was alone —abandoned by the very ones whom He had chosen as witnesses to, and companions of, His life, and whom He had loved unto the end (Jn. 13:1), but He stated, "I am not alone, for the Father is with me" (Jn. 16:22). He who has

chosen to belong completely to Christ will find, above all, in intimacy with Him and in His grace, the power of spirit necessary to banish sadness and regret and to triumph over discouragement. He will not be lacking the protection of the Virgin Mother of Jesus nor the motherly solicitude of the Church, to whom he has given himself in service. He will not be without the kindly care of his father in Christ, the bishop; nor will the fraternal companionship of his fellow priests and the comfort of the entire People of God be lacking to him. And if hostility, lack of confidence and the indifference of his fellowmen make his solitude quite painful, he will thus be able to share, with dramatic clarity, the very experience of Christ, as an apostle who is not above Him by whom he has been sent (cf. Jn. 13:16, 14:18), as a friend admitted to the most painful and most glorious secret of his divine Friend who has chosen him to bring forth the mysterious fruit of life in his own life, which is only apparently one of death (cf. Jn. 15:15-16, 20).

SECOND PART

I. Priestly Formation

An Adequate Formation

60. Our reflection on the beauty, importance and intimate fittingness of holy virginity for the ministers of Christ and His Church makes it incumbent on the Teacher and Pastor of that

Church to assure and promote its positive observance, from the first moment of preparation to receive such a precious gift.

In fact, the difficulties and problems which make the observance of chastity very painful or quite impossible for some, spring, not infrequently, from a type of priestly formation which, given the great changes of these last years, is no longer completely adequate for the formation of a personality worthy of a *man of God* (1 Tm. 6:11).

The Execution of the Norms of the Council

61. The Second Vatican Council has already indicated wise criteria and guidelines to this end. They are in conformity with the progress of psychology and pedagogy as well as with the changed conditions of mankind and of contemporary society.[37] It is our will that apposite instructions be drawn up with the help of truly qualified men treating with all necessary detail the theme of chastity. They should be sent out as soon as possible to provide those who, within the Church, have the great responsibility of preparing future priests, with competent and timely assistance.

Personal Response to the Divine Vocation

62. The priesthood is a ministry instituted by Christ for the service of His Mystical Body which is the Church. To her belongs the authority to admit to that priesthood those whom she judges qualified: that is, those to whom God

has given, along with other signs of an ecclesiastical vocation, the gift of a consecrated celibacy (cf. #15).

In virtue of such a gift, corroborated by canon law, the individual is called to respond with free judgment and total dedication, subordinating his own ego to the will of God who calls him. Concretely, this divine calling manifests itself in a given individual with his own definite personality structure which under normal circumstances is not violently mastered by grace. In the candidates for the priesthood, therefore, the sense of receiving this divine gift should be cultivated; so too a sense of responsibility in their meeting with God, with the highest importance given to supernatural means.

The Plane of Grace and the Plane of Nature

63. It is likewise necessary that exact account be taken of the biological and psychological state of the candidate in order to guide and orient him toward the priestly ideal; so a truly adequate formation should coordinate harmoniously grace and nature in the man in whom one clearly sees the objective conditions and effective capability of receiving the gift of chastity. These conditions should be ascertained as soon as signs of his holy vocation are first indicated; not hastily or superficially, but carefully, with the assistance and aid of a doctor and of a competent psychologist. A serious investigation of hereditary factors should not be omitted.

The Unfit

64. Those who are discovered to be unfit—either for physical, psychological or moral reasons—should be quickly removed from the path to the priesthood. Let educators appreciate that this is one of their very grave duties. Let them not abandon themselves to false hopes and to dangerous illusions and let them not permit the candidate to nourish these hopes in any way, with resultant damage either to himself or to the Church. The life of the celibate priest, which engages the whole man so totally and so delicately, excludes in fact those of insufficient psycho-physical and moral balance. Nor should anyone pretend that grace supplies for the defects of nature in such a man.

Development of the Personality

65. After the capability of a man has been ascertained and he has been admitted to the course of studies leading to the goal of the priesthood, care should be taken for the progressive development of his personality through the means of physical, intellectual and moral education directed toward the control and personal dominion of his instincts, sentiments and passions.

The Necessity of Discipline

66. This will be proved by the firmness of the spirit with which he accepts the personal and community type of discipline demanded by the priestly life. Such a regime, the lack or deficiency of which is to be deplored because it exposes the

candidate to grave dangers, should not be borne only as an imposition from without. It should be interiorized and implanted within the context of the spiritual life as an indispensable component.

Personal Initiative

67. The educator should skillfully stimulate the young man to that totally evangelical virtue of sincerity (cf. Mt. 5:37) and to spontaneity by approving of every good personal initiative, so that he will come to know, and properly evaluate himself, assume wisely his own responsibilities, and train himself to that self-control which is of such importance in the priestly education.

The Exercise of Authority

68. The exercise of authority, the principle of which ought to be held to firmly, will be animated by wise moderation and by a pastoral attitude. It will be used in a climate of dialogue and will be implemented in a gradual way which will afford the educator an ever deepening understanding of the psychology of the young man, and will appeal to personal conviction.

Conscious Choice

69. The complete education of the candidate to the priesthood ought to be directed to help him acquire a tranquil, convinced and free choice of the grave responsibilities which he must assume in conscience before God and the Church. Ardor and generosity are marvelous qualities of youth; illuminated and supported, they merit, along with the blessing of the Lord, the admiration and

confidence of the whole Church as well as of all men. None of the real personal and social difficulties which their choice will bring in its train should remain hidden to the young men so that their enthusiasm will not be superficial and illusory. At the same time it will be right to highlight with at least equal truth and clarity the sublimity of their choice, which on the one hand leads to a certain physical and psychic void but on the other, brings with it an interior richness capable of elevating the person most profoundly.

An Asceticism for the Maturation of the Personality

70. The young candidates for the priesthood should convince themselves that they are not able to follow their difficult way without a special type of asceticism more demanding than that which is asked of all the other faithful, which is proper to themselves. It will be a demanding asceticism but not a suffocating one which consists in the deliberate and assiduous practice of those virtues which make a man a priest: self-denial in the highest degree—an essential condition if one would follow Christ (Mt. 16:24, Jn. 12:25), humility and obedience as expressions of internal truth and of a guided liberty; prudence, justice, courage and temperance, virtues without which it is impossible for true and profound religious life to exist; a sense of responsibility, of fidelity and of loyalty in the acceptance of one's obligations; a balance between contemplation and action; detachment and a spirit of poverty which will give tone and vigor to evangelical

freedom; chastity, the result of a persevering struggle, harmonized with all the other natural and supernatural virtues; a serene and secure contact with the world for the service of which the young man will dedicate himself for Christ and for His kingdom.

In such a way the aspirant to the priesthood will acquire, with the help of divine grace, a balanced personality, strong and mature, a combination of inherited and acquired qualities, harmony of all of his powers in the light of the faith and in intimate union with Christ, whom he has chosen for himself and for the ministry of salvation to the world.

Periods of Experimentation

71. However, to judge with better certainty the fitness of the young man for the priesthood and to have successive proofs of his attained maturity on both the human and supernatural levels, in consideration of the fact that "it is more difficult to conduct oneself correctly in the service of souls because of dangers coming from outside,"[38] it will be advisable to have the obligation of holy celibacy observed during specified periods of experimentation before it becomes something stable and definitive with the priesthood.[39]

The Choice of Celibacy as of a Gift

72. Once moral certainty has been obtained that the maturity of the candidate is sufficiently guaranteed, he will be in a position to take on himself the heavy and sweet burden of sacerdotal chastity as a total gift of himself to the Lord and to His Church.

In this way the obligation of celibacy, which the Church adds as an objective condition to Holy Orders, becomes the candidate's own accepted personal obligation under the influence of divine grace and with full reflection and liberty, and evidently not without the wise and prudent advice of competent spiritual directors who are concerned not to impose the choice, but rather to dispose the candidate to become more conscious in his choice.

Hence, in that solemn moment when the candidate will decide once and for his whole life, he will not feel the weight of an imposition from outside, but rather the interior joy that accompanies a choice made for the love of Christ.

II. The Priestly Life

An Unending Conquest

73. The priest must not think that ordination makes everything easy for him and screens him once for all from every temptation or danger. Chastity is not acquired all at once but results from a laborious conquest and daily affirmation. Our world today stresses the positive values of love between the sexes but has also multiplied the difficulties and risks in this sphere. In order to safeguard his chastity with all care and affirm its sublime meaning, the priest must consider clearly and calmly his position as a man exposed to spiritual warfare against the seductions of the flesh in himself and in the world, continually renewing his resolution to give an ever increasing

and ever better perfection to the irrevocable offering of himself which obliges him to a fidelity that is complete, loyal and real.

Supernatural Means

74. Christ's priest will receive new strength and joy daily as he deepens in his meditation and prayer the motives for his gift and the conviction that he has chosen the better part. He will ask humbly and perseveringly for the grace of fidelity, never denied to those who ask it sincerely. At the same time he will use the natural and supernatural means at his disposal. In particular he will not disregard those ascetical norms, guaranteed by the Church's experience and no less necessary in modern circumstances than in former times.[40]

Intense Spiritual Life

75. The priest should apply himself above all else to developing, with all the love grace inspires in him, his close relationship with Christ, searching the inexhaustible and enriching mystery; he should also acquire an ever deeper sense of the mystery of the Church. There would be the risk of his state of life seeming unreasonable and unfounded if seen apart from this mystery.

Priestly piety, nourished at the table of God's Word and the Holy Eucharist, lived within the cycle of the liturgical year, inspired by a warm and enlightened devotion to the Virgin Mother of the Supreme and Eternal High Priest and Queen of the Apostles,[41] will bring him to the source of a true spiritual life which alone provides a solid foundation for the observance of celibacy.

The Spirit of the Priestly Ministry

76. In this way the priest with grace and peace in his heart will face with generosity the manifold tasks of his life and ministry. If he performs these with faith and zeal he will find in them new occasions to show that he belongs entirely to Christ and His Mystical Body, for his own sanctification and the sanctification of others. The charity of Christ which urges him on (2 Cor. 5:14) will help him not to renounce his higher feelings but to elevate and deepen them in a spirit of consecration in imitation of Christ the High Priest, who shared intimately in the life of mankind, loved and suffered for them (Heb. 4:15), and of Paul the Apostle who shared in the cares of all (1 Cor. 9:22; 2 Cor. 11:29), in order to bring the light and power of the Gospel of God's grace to shine in the world (Acts 20:24).

Defense Against Dangers

77. Rightly jealous of his full self-giving to the Lord, the priest should know how to guard against sentimental tendencies which imperil an affectivity not sufficiently enlightened or guided by the Spirit. He should beware of looking for spiritual or apostolic pretexts for what are in fact dangerous inclinations of the heart.

Virile Asceticism

78. The priestly life certainly requires an authentic spiritual intensity in order to live by

the Spirit and to conform to the Spirit (Gal. 5:25); it requires a truly virile asceticism both interior and exterior in one who, belonging in a special way to Christ, has in Him and through Him crucified the flesh with its passions and desires (Gal. 5:24), not hesitating to face arduous and lengthy trials in order to do so (cf. 1 Cor. 9:26-27). In this way Christ's minister will be the better able to show to the world the fruits of the Spirit which are "love, joy, peace, patience, kindness, goodness, long-suffering, mildness, faithfulness, gentleness, self-control, chastity" (Gal. 5:22-23).

The Brotherhood of Priests

79. Moreover, priestly chastity is increased, guarded and defended by a way of life, surroundings and activity suited to a minister of God. For this reason the "close sacramental brotherhood"[42] which all priests enjoy in virtue of their ordination must be fostered to the utmost. Our Lord Jesus Christ has taught the urgency of the new commandment of charity. He gave a wonderful example of it when He instituted the sacrament of the Eucharist and the Catholic priesthood (Jn. 13:15, 34-35), and prayed to His heavenly Father that the love the Father bore for Him from all eternity should be in His ministers and that He too should be in them (Jn. 17:26).

Unity of Priests in Spirit and Life

80. So the unity of spirit among priests should be perfect and they should be active in their prayers, friendship and help of all kinds for one another. One cannot sufficiently recommend

to priests a life lived in common and directed entirely toward their sacred ministry; the practice of having frequent meetings with a fraternal exchange of ideas, counsel and experience with their brother priests; the movement to form associations which encourage priestly holiness.

Charity for Fellow Priests in Danger

81. Priests should reflect on the advice of the Council[43] which reminds them of their common sharing in the priesthood so that they may feel a lively responsibility for fellow priests troubled by difficulties which gravely endanger the divine gift they have. They should have a burning charity for those who have greater need of love, understanding and prayer, who have need of prudent but effective help, and who have a claim on their unbounded charity as those who are, and should be, their truest friends.

Renewal of the Choice

82. Venerable brothers in the episcopacy, priests and ministers of the altar, by way of completing and leaving a remembrance of this written conversation with you, we should like to suggest this resolution to you: that on the anniversary of his ordination, or on Holy Thursday when all are united in spirit commemorating the mystery of the institution of the priesthood, each one should renew his total gift of himself to Christ our Lord; reviving in this way the awareness that He has chosen you for His divine service, and repeating at the same time, humbly and courageously, the promise you have made of

unswerving faithfulness to His love alone in your offering of perfect chastity (cf. Rom. 12:1).

III. Lamentable Defections

True Responsibility

83. Now with fatherly love and affection, our heart turns anxiously and with deep sorrow to those unfortunate priests who always remain our dearly beloved brothers and whose misfortune we keenly regret: those who, retaining the sacred character conferred by their priestly ordination, have been or are unfortunately unfaithful to the obligations they accepted when they were ordained.

Their sad state and its consequences to priests and to others move some to wonder if celibacy is not in some way responsible for such dramatic occurrences and for the scandals they inflict on God's People. In fact, the responsibility falls not on consecrated celibacy in itself but on a judgment of the fitness of the candidate for the priesthood which was not always adequate or prudent at the proper time, or else it falls on the way in which sacred ministers live their life of total consecration.

Reasons for Dispensations

84. The Church is very conscious of the sad state of these sons of hers and judges it necessary to make every effort to avert or to remedy the wounds she suffers by their defection. Following the example of our immediate Predecessors of holy memory, we also have, in cases concerning

ordination to the priesthood, been prepared to allow inquiry to extend beyond the provisions of the present canon law (cf. C.I.C. can. 214) to other very grave reasons which give ground for really solid doubts regarding the full freedom and responsibility of the candidate for the priesthood and his fitness for the priestly state. This has been done to free those who, on careful judicial consideration of their case, are seen to be really unsuited.

The Church's Justice and Charity

85. The dispensations which are granted after such consideration—a minimal percentage when they are compared with the great number of good, worthy priests—provide in justice for the spiritual salvation of the individual and show at the same time the Church's concern to safeguard celibacy and the complete fidelity of all her ministers. In granting such dispensations the Church always acts with heartfelt regret, especially in the particularly lamentable cases in which refusal to bear worthily this sweet yoke of Christ results from crises in faith, or moral weakness, and is thus frequently a failure in responsibility and a scandal.

An Heartrending Appeal

86. If these priests knew how much sorrow, dishonor and unrest they bring to the holy Church of God; if they reflected on the seriousness and the beauty of their obligations and on the dangers to which they are exposed in this life and in the next, there would be greater care and

reflection in their decisions, they would pray more assiduously, and would show greater courage and logic in forestalling the causes of their spiritual and moral collapse.

The Church's Motherly Care

87. The Church has particular interest in those young priests who are on the threshold of their ministry and full of zeal and enthusiasm. Because of the tensions to which their priestly obligations are subject, is it not to be expected that they will experience moments of diffidence, doubt, passion, folly? Hence, it is the wish of the Church that every persuasive means available be used to lead them from this wavering state to one of calm, trust, penance, recovery. It is only when no other solution can be found for a priest in this unhappy condition that he should be relieved of his office.

The Granting of Dispensations

88. There are some whose priesthood cannot be saved, but whose serious dispositions nevertheless give promise of their being able to live as good Christian lay people. To these the Holy See, having studied all the circumstances with their bishops or with their religious superiors, sometimes grants a dispensation, thus letting love conquer sorrow. In order, however, that her unhappy but always dear son may have a salutary sign of her maternal grief and a keener remembrance of the universal need of God's mercy, in these cases she imposes some works of piety and reparation.

Encouragement and Warnings

89. Inspiring this discipline, which is at once severe and merciful, are justice and truth, prudence and reserve. It is without doubt a discipline which will confirm good priests in their determination to live lives of purity and holiness. At the same time it will be a warning to those aspiring to the priesthood. These, guided by the wisdom of those who educate them, will approach their priesthood fully aware of its obligations, disinterested and responding generously to divine grace and the will of Christ and His Church.

Consolations

90. Finally and with deep joy, we thank our Lord because many priests, who for a time had been unfaithful to their obligations, have with the grace of the High Priest found again the path and given joy to all by becoming anew exemplary pastors. With admirable good will, they used all the means which were helpful to ensure their return, especially an intense life of prayer, humility, persevering effort sustained by regular reception of the Sacrament of Penance.

IV. The Bishop's Fatherliness

The Bishop and His Priests

91. There is an irreplaceable and very effective means to ensure for our dear priests an easier and happier way of being faithful to their obliga-

tions, and it is one which they have the right and duty to find in you, venerable brother bishops. It was you who called them and destined them to be priests; it was you who placed your hands on their heads; with you they are one in sharing the honor of the priesthood by virtue of the Sacrament of Orders; it is you whom they make present in the community of the faithful; with you they are united in a spirit of trust and magnanimity since, in as far as is compatible with their order, they take upon themselves your duties and care.[44] In choosing a life dedicated to celibacy they follow the ancient examples of the prelates of the East and the West; this provides a new motive for union between bishop and priest and a sound hope that they will live together more closely.

Responsibility and Pastoral Love

92. The affection which Jesus had for His Apostles showed itself very clearly when He made them ministers of His real and Mystical Body (cf. Jn. 13-17); and even you in whose person "Our Lord Jesus Christ, the Supreme High Priest, is present in the midst of those who believe"[45] know that you owe the best part of your hearts and pastoral care to your priests and to the young men preparing to be priests.[46] In no other way can you better show this conviction than in the conscious responsibility and sincere and unconquerable love with which you preside over the education of your seminarians, and help your priests in every way possible to remain faithful to their vocation and their duties.

A Bishop's Kindness

93. It is your fraternal and kindly presence and deeds that must fill up in advance the human loneliness of the priest, which is so often the cause of his discouragement and temptations.[47] Before being the superiors and judges of your priests, be their masters, fathers, friends, their good and kind brothers always ready to understand, to sympathize and to help. In every possible way encourage your priests to be your personal friends and to be very open with you. This will not weaken the relationship of juridical obedience; rather it will transform it into pastoral love so that they will obey more willingly, sincerely and securely. If they are your devoted friends and if they have a filial trust in you, your priests will be able in time to open up their souls and to confide in you their difficulties in the certainty that they can rely on your kindness to be protected from eventual defeat, without a servile fear of punishment, but in the filial expectation of correction, pardon and help, which will inspire them to resume their difficult journey with a new confidence.

Authority and Fatherliness

94. Venerable brothers, all of you are certainly convinced that to restore to the soul of a priest joy in and enthusiasm for his vocation, interior peace and salvation is an urgent and glorious ministry which has an incalculable influence on a multitude of souls. There will be times when you must exercise your authority by showing a just severity towards those few who,

after having resisted your kindness, by their conduct cause scandal to the People of God; but you will take the necessary precautions to ensure their seeing the error of their ways. Following the example of our Lord Jesus, the Pastor and Bishop of our souls (1 Pt. 2:25), do not crush the bruised reed nor quench the smoking flax (Mt. 12:20); like Jesus, heal their wounds (cf. 9:12), save what was lost (cf. Mt. 18:11), with eagerness and love go in search of the lost sheep and bring him back to the warmth of the sheepfold (cf. Lk. 15:4ff.) and, like Him, try until the end (cf. Lk. 22:48) to call back the faithful friend.

Teaching and Vigilance

95. We are certain, venerable brothers, that you will leave nothing undone to foster, by your teaching, prudence and pastoral zeal, the ideal of consecrated celibacy among your clergy. We are sure too that you will never neglect those priests who have strayed from the house of God, their true home, no matter where their painful odyssey has led them, since they still remain your sons.

V. Role of the Faithful

Responsibility of the Entire People of God

96. Priestly virtue is a treasure that belongs to the whole Church. It is an enrichment and a splendor above the ordinary, which redounds to the building up and the profit of the entire People of God. We wish therefore to address to all the faithful, our children in Christ, an affectionate

and urgent exhortation. We wish that they too feel responsible for the virtue of those brothers of theirs who have undertaken the mission of serving them in the priesthood for the salvation of their souls. They should pray and work for priestly vocations; they should help priests wholeheartedly, with filial love and ready collaboration; they should have the firm intention of offering them the consolation of a joyous response to their pastoral labors. They should encourage these, their fathers in Christ, to overcome the difficulties of every sort which they encounter as they fulfill their duties with entire faithfulness, to the edification of all. They should foster in a spirit of faith and of Christian love a deep respect and a delicate reserve in their dealings with priests, on account of their condition as men entirely consecrated to Christ and to the Church.

Invitation to the Laity

97. Our invitation goes out specially to those lay people who seek God with greater earnestness and intensity, and strive after Christian perfection while living in the midst of their fellowmen. By their devoted and warm friendship they can be of great assistance to the Church's ministers since it is the laity, occupied with temporal affairs while at the same time aiming at a more generous and more perfect response to their baptismal vocation, who are in a position, in many cases, to enlighten and encourage the priest. Moreover, the perfect response to a vocation that plunges him into the

mystery of Christ and the Church can suffer harm from various circumstances and from contamination with a certain kind of worldliness. In this way the whole People of God will honor Christ our Lord in those who represent Him and of whom He has said: "He who receives you receives me, and he who receives me receives him who sent me" (Mt. 10:40), promising an assured reward to whoever in any way shows charity toward those whom He has sent *(ibid.,* v. 42).

Conclusion

Mary's Intercession

98. Venerable brothers, pastors of God's flock throughout the world, and dearly beloved priests, our sons and brothers: as we come to the end of this letter which we have addressed to you, we invite you, with a soul responsive to Christ's great love, to turn your eyes and heart with renewed confidence and filial hope to the most loving Mother of Jesus and Mother of the Church, and to invoke for the Catholic priesthood her powerful and maternal intercession. In her the People of God admire and venerate the image of the Church, and model of faith, charity and perfect union with Him. May Mary, Virgin and Mother, obtain for the Church, which also is hailed as virgin and mother,[48] to rejoice always, though with due humility, in the faithfulness of her priests to the sublime gift they have received of holy virginity, and to see it flourishing and appreciated ever more and more in every walk of

life, so that the army of those who follow the divine Lamb wherever He goes (cf. Rv. 14:4) may increase throughout the earth.

Confident Hope of the Church

99. The Church proclaims her hope in Christ; she is conscious of the critical shortage of priests when compared with the spiritual necessities of the world's population; but she is confident in her expectation which is founded on the infinite and mysterious power of grace, that the high spiritual quality of her ministers will bring about an increase also in their numbers, for everything is possible to God (cf. Mk. 10:27, Lk. 1:37).

In this faith and in this hope, may the apostolic blessing which we impart with all our heart be for all a pledge of heavenly graces and the testimony of our fatherly affection.

Rome, at St. Peter's, June 24, 1967, feast of St. John the Baptist, fifth year of our Pontificate.

Pope Paul VI

FOOTNOTES

1. Letter of Oct. 10, 1965 to H. E. Card. E. Tisserant, read in the 146th General Congregation on Oct. 11.
2. Second Vatican Ecumenical Council, Decree *Christus Dominus*, no. 35; *Apostolicam actuositatem*, no. 1; *Presbyterorum ordinis*, nos. 10, 11; *Ad gentes*, nos. 19, 38.
3. Second Vatican Ecumenical Council, Constitution *Gaudium et spes*, no. 62.
4. Decree *Presbyterorum ordinis*, no. 16.
5. Second Vatican Ecumenical Council, Dogmatic Constitution *Dei Verbum*, no. 8.

PRIESTLY CELIBACY 69

6. Second Vatican Ecumenical Council, Dogmatic Constitution *Lumen gentium*, no. 28; Decree *Presbyterorum ordinis*, no. 2.
7. Decree *Presbyterorum ordinis*, no. 16.
8. Decree *Presbyterorum ordinis*, no. 16.
9. Constitution *Lumen gentium*, no. 42.
10. Cf. Dogmatic Constitution *Lumen gentium*, no. 42; Decree *Presbyterorum ordinis*, no. 16.
11. Decree *Presbyterorum ordinis*, no. 14.
12. Cf. Decree *Presbyterorum ordinis*, no. 13.
13. Decree *Presbyterorum ordinis*, no. 5.
14. Decree *Optatam totius*, no. 10.
15. Decree *Presbyterorum ordinis*, no. 16.
16. Pastoral Constitution *Gaudium et spes*, no. 39.
17. Dogmatic Constitution *Lumen gentium*, no. 5.
18. Dogmatic Constitution *Lumen gentium*, no. 48.
19. Second Vatican Ecumenical Council, Decree *Perfectae caritatis*, no. 12.
20. Cf. Tertullian, *De exhort. castitatis*, 13: PL 2, 930; St. Epiphanius, *Adv. haer.* II, 48, 9 and 59, 4: PG 41, 869, 1025; St. Ephrem, *Carmina nisibena*, XVIII, XIX, ed. G. Bickell, Leipzig, 1866, p. 122; Eusebius of Caesarea, *Demonstr. evang.* 1, 9; PG 22, 81; St. Cyril of Jerusalem, *Catech.* 12, 25: PG 33, 757; St. Ambrose, *De offic. ministr.* 1, 50: PL 16, 97ff.; St. Augustine, *De moribus Eccl. cathol.* 1, 32: PL 32, E399; St. Jerome, *Adv. Vigilant.* 2: PL 23, 340-41; Sinesius, Bishop of Ptolemais, *Epist.* 105: PG 66, 1485.
21. The first time in the Council of Elvira in Spain (c. a. 300), c. 33: Mansi II, 11.
22. Session XXIV, can. 9-10.
23. St. Pius X, Exhortation *Haerent animo*, Aug. 4, 1908: AAS 41, 1908, pp. 555-557; Benedict XV, Letter to F. Kordac, Archbishop of Prague, Jan. 29, 1920: AAS 12, 1920, p. 57f.; *Consist. Alloc.* Dec. 16, 1920: AAS 12, 1920, pp. 585-588; Pius XI, Encyclical *Ad catholici sacerdotii*, Dec. 20, 1935: AAS 28, 1936, pp. 24-30; Pius XII, Apostolic Exhortation *Menti nostrae*, Sept. 23, 1950: AAS 42, 1950, pp. 657-702; Encyclical *Sacra virginitas*, March 25, 1954: AAS 46, 1954, pp. 161-191; John XXIII, Encyclical *Sacerdotii nostri primordia*, Aug. 1, 1959: AAS 51, pp. 554-556.
24. Second Allocution to the Roman Synod. Jan. 26, 1960: AAS 52, 1960, pp. 235-236 (Latin text p. 226).
25. Can. 6, 12, 13, 48: Mansi XI, 944-948, 965.
26. Decree *Presbyterorum ordinis*, no. 16.

27. Decree *De virginitate*, 13: PG 46, 381-382.
28. *De sacerdotio*, 1. III, 4: PG 48, 642.
29. Dogmatic Constitution *Lumen gentium*, nos. 21, 28, 64.
30. Constitution cit., no. 29.
31. Constitution cit., no. 49.
32. Decree *Presbyterorum ordinis*, no. 16.
33. Decree *Optatam totius*, no. 2; *Presbyterorum ordinis*, no. 11.
34. Confess. X, 29, 40: PL 32, 796.
35. Cf. 1 Thes. 2, 11; 1 Cor. 4:15; 2 Cor. 6:13; Gal. 4:19; 1 Tm. 5:1-2.
36. Decree *Presbyterorum ordinis*, no. 3.
37. Decree *Optatam totius*, nos. 3-11; cf. *Perfectae caritatis*, no. 12.
38. St. Thomas Aquinas, Summa th. IIa-IIae, q. 184, a. 8 c.
39. Decree *Optatam totius*, no. 12.
40. Decree *Presbyterorum ordinis*, nos. 16, 18.
41. Decree *Presbyterorum ordinis*, no. 18.
42. Decree *Presbyterorum ordinis*, no. 8.
43. Decree cit., *ibid.*
44. Dogmatic Constitution *Lumen gentium*, no. 28.
45. Dogmatic Constitution *Lumen gentium*, no. 21.
46. Decree *Presbyterorum ordinis*, no. 7.
47. Decree cit., *ibid.*
48. Dogmatic Constitution *Lumen gentium*, nos. 63, 64.

POPE JOHN PAUL II

To All Bishops of the Church

On the occasion of Holy Thursday, 1979.

Venerable brothers in the episcopate,

The great day is drawing near when we shall share in the liturgy of Holy Thursday together with our brothers in the priesthood and shall meditate together on the priceless gift in which we have become sharers by virtue of the call of Christ the eternal Priest. On that day, before we celebrate the liturgy *In Cena Domini,* we shall gather together in our cathedrals to renew before Him who became for us "obedient unto death"[1] in total self-giving to the Church, His spouse, our giving of ourselves to the exclusive service of Christ in His Church.

On this holy day, the liturgy takes us inside the Upper Room, where, with grateful heart, we set ourselves to listen to the words of the divine Teacher, words full of solicitude for every generation of bishops called, after the Apostles, to take upon themselves care for the Church, for the flock, for the vocation of the whole People of God, for the proclamation of God's Word, for the whole sacramental and moral order of Christian living, for priestly and religious vocations, for the fraternal spirit in the community. Christ says: "I will not leave you orphans; I will come back to you."[2] It is precisely this Sacred Triduum of the passion, death and resurrection of the Lord that re-evokes in us, in a vivid way, not only the memory of His departure, but also faith in His return, in His continuous coming. Indeed, what is the meaning of the words: "I am with you always; yes, to the end of time"?[3]

Venerable and dear brothers, in the spirit of this faith, which fills the entire Triduum, it is my desire that, in our vocation and our episcopal ministry, we should feel in a special way this year—the first of my pontificate—that unity which the Twelve shared in when together with our Lord they were assembled for the Last Supper. It was precisely there that they heard those words that were most complimentary and at the same time most binding: "I shall not call you servants any more, because a servant does not know his master's business; I call you friends, because I have made known to you everything I have learned from my Father. You did not choose me, no, I chose you; and I commissioned you to go out and to bear fruit, fruit that will last."[4]

Can anything be added to those words? Should one not rather pause in humility and gratitude before them, given the greatness of the mystery we are about to celebrate? There then takes root even deeper within us our awareness of the gift that we have received from the Lord through our vocation and our episcopal ordination. In fact the gift of the sacramental fullness of the priesthood is greater than all the toils and also all the sufferings involved in our pastoral ministry in the episcopate.

The Second Vatican Council reminded us and clearly showed us that this ministry, while being a personal duty of each one of us, is nevertheless something that we carry out in the brotherly communion of the whole of the Church's episcopal college or "body." While it is right that we should address every human being, and especially every Christian as "brother," this word takes on an altogether special meaning with regard to us bishops and our mutual relationship: in a certain sense it goes back directly to that brotherhood which gathered the Apostles about Christ; it goes back to that friendship with which Christ honored them and through which He united them to one another, as is attested by the words of John's Gospel quoted above.

Therefore, venerable and dear brothers, we must express the wish, today especially, that everything that the Second Vatican Council so wonderfully renewed in our awareness should take on an ever more mature character of collegiality, both as the principle of our collaboration *(collegialitas effectiva)* and as the character of a cordial fraternal bond *(collegialitas affectiva)*, in order to build up the Mystical Body of Christ and to deepen the unity of the whole People of God.

As you gather in your cathedrals, with the diocesan and religious priests who make up the *presbyterium* of your local Churches, your dioceses, you will receive from them—as is provided for—the renewal of the promises that they placed in the hands of you, the bishops, on the day of their priestly ordination. With this in mind, I am sending to the priests another letter that—as I hope—will enable you and them to live even more deeply this unity, this mysterious bond that joins us in the one priesthood of Jesus Christ, brought to completion with the sacrifice of the cross, which merited for Him entrance "into the sanctuary."[5] Venerable brothers, I hope that these words of mine addressed to the priests, at the beginning of my ministry in the See of St. Peter, will also help you to strengthen ever more that communion and unity of the whole *presbyterium*[6] which have their basis in our collegial communion and unity in the Church.

And may there be a renewal of your love for the priests whom the Holy Spirit has given and entrusted to you as the closest collaborators in your pastoral office. Take care of them like beloved sons, brothers and friends. Be mindful of all their needs. Have particular solicitude for their spiritual advancement, for their perseverance in the grace of the sacrament of the priesthood. Since it is into your hands they make—and each year renew—their priestly promises, and especially the commitment to celibacy, do everything in your power to ensure that they remain faithful to these promises, as is demanded by the holy tradition of the Church, the tradition that sprang from the very spirit of the Gospel.

May this solicitude for our brothers in the priestly ministry also be extended to the seminaries, which constitute, in the Church as a whole and in each of her parts, an eloquent proof of her vitality and spiritual fruitfulness, which are expressed precisely in readiness to give oneself exclusively to the service of God and of souls. Today, every possible effort must again be made to encourage vocations, to form new generations of priests. This must be done in a genuinely evangelical spirit, and at the same time by "reading" properly the signs of the times, to which the Second Vatican Council gave such careful attention. The full reconstitution of the life of the seminaries throughout the Church will be the best proof of the achievement of the renewal to which the Council directed the Church.

Venerable and dear brothers: everything that I am writing to you, as I prepare to live Holy Thursday intensely—the "feast of priests"—I wish to link up closely with the desire that the Apostles heard expressed that day by the lips of their beloved Teacher: "Go out and bear fruit, fruit that will last."[7] We can bear this fruit only if we remain in Him: in the vine.[8] He told us this clearly in His words of farewell on the day before His Passover: "Whoever remains in me, with me in him, bears fruit in plenty; for cut off from me you can do nothing."[9] Beloved brothers, what more could I wish you, what more could we wish one another, than precisely this: to remain in Him, Jesus Christ, and to bear fruit, fruit that will last?

Accept these good wishes. Let us strive to deepen ever more our unity; let us strive to live ever more intensely the sacred Triduum of the Passover of our Lord Jesus Christ.

From the Vatican, April 8, Passion Sunday (Palm Sunday), in the year 1979, the first of the Pontificate.

Pope John Paul II

FOOTNOTES

1. Phil. 2:8.
2. Jn. 14:18.
3. Mt. 28:20.
4. Jn. 15:15-16.
5. Cf. Heb. 9:12.
6. Cf. Dogmatic Constitution *Lumen gentium*, no. 28.
7. Jn. 15:16.
8. Cf. Jn. 15:1-8.
9. Jn. 15:5.

To All the Priests of the Church

On the occasion of Holy Thursday, 1979.

For You I Am a Bishop, with You I Am a Priest

Dear brother priests,

1. At the beginning of my new ministry in the Church, I feel the deep need to speak to you, to all of you without any exception, priests both diocesan and religious, who are my brothers by virtue of the sacrament of Orders. From the very beginning I wish to express my faith in the vocation that unites you to your bishops, in a special communion of sacrament and ministry, through which the Church, the Mystical Body of Christ, is built up. To all of you, therefore, who, by virtue of a special grace and through a singular gift of our Savior, bear "the burden of the day and the heat"[1] in the midst of the many tasks of the priestly and pastoral ministry, I have addressed my thoughts and my heart from the moment when Christ called me to this See, where Saint Peter, with his life and his death, had to respond until the end to the question: Do you love me? Do you love me more than these others do?[2]

I think of you all the time, I pray for you, with you *I seek the ways of spiritual union and collaboration*, because by virtue of the sacrament of Orders, which I also received from the hands of my bishop (the Metropolitan of Krakow, Cardinal Adam Stephen Sapieha, of unforgettable memory), you are my brothers. And so, adapting the words of St. Augustine,[3] I want to say to you today: "For you I am a bishop, with you I am a priest." Today, in fact, there is a special circumstance that impels me to confide to you some thoughts that I enclose in this Letter: it is the nearness of Holy Thursday. It is this, the annual feast of our priesthood, that unites the whole presbyterium of each diocese about its bishop in the shared celebration of the Eucharist. It is on this day that all priests are invited to renew, before their own bishop and together with him, the promises they made at their priestly ordination; and this fact enables me, together with all my brothers in the episcopate, to be joined to you in a special unity, and especially to be in the very heart of the mystery of Jesus Christ, the mystery in which we all share.

The Second Vatican Council, which so explicitly highlighted the collegiality of the episcopate in the Church, also gave a new form to the life of the priestly communities, joined together by a special bond of brotherhood, and united to the bishop of the respective local Church. The whole priestly life and ministry serve to deepen and strengthen that bond; and a particular responsibility for the various tasks involved by this life and ministry is taken on by the priests' councils, which, in conformity with the thought of the Council and the Motu Proprio *Ecclesiae sanctae*[4] of Paul VI, should be functioning in every diocese. All this is meant to ensure that each bishop, in union with his presbyterium, can serve ever more effectively the great cause of evangelization. Through this service the Church realizes her mission, indeed her very nature. The importance of the unity of the priests with their own bishop on this point is confirmed by the words of St. Ignatius of Antioch: "Strive to do all things in the harmony of God, with the bishop presiding to represent God, the presbyters representing the council of the apostles, and the deacons, so dear to me, entrusted with the service of Jesus Christ."[5]

Love for Christ and the Church Unites Us

2. It is not my intention to include in this Letter everything that makes up the richness of the priestly life and ministry. In this regard I refer to the whole tradition of the Magisterium and of the Church, and in a special way to the doctrine of the Second Vatican Council, contained in the Council's various documents, especially in the Constitution *Lumen gentium* and the Decrees *Presbyterorum ordinis* and *Ad gentes.* I also wish to recall the Encyclical of my Predecessor Paul VI, *Sacerdotalis caelibatus.* Finally, I wish to place great importance upon the Document *De sacerdotio ministeriali,* which Paul VI approved as the fruit of the labors of the 1971 Synod of Bishops, because I find in this document—although

the session of the Synod that elaborated it had only a consultative form—a statement of essential importance regarding the specific aspect of the priestly life and ministry in the modern world.

Referring to all these sources, which you are familiar with, I wish in the present Letter *only to mention a number of points* which seem to me to be of extreme importance at this moment in the history of the Church and of the world. These are words that are dictated to me by my love for the Church, which will be able to carry out her mission to the world only if—in spite of all human weakness—she maintains her fidelity to Christ. I know that I am addressing those whom only the love of Christ has enabled, by means of a specific vocation, to give themselves to the service of the Church and, in the Church, to the service of man for the solution of the most important problems, and especially those regarding man's eternal salvation.

Although at the beginning of these considerations I refer to many written sources and official documents, nevertheless I wish to refer especially to that living source which is our shared love for Christ and His Church, a love that springs from the grace of the priestly vocation, the love that is the greatest gift of the Holy Spirit.[6]

"Chosen from Among Men... Appointed To Act on Behalf of Men"[7]

3. The Second Vatican Council deepened the idea of the priesthood and presented it,

throughout its teaching, as the expression of the inner forces, those "dynamisms," whereby the mission of the whole People of God in the Church is constituted. Here one should refer especially to the Constitution *Lumen gentium*, and reread carefully the relevant paragraphs. The mission of the People of God is carried out through the sharing in the office and mission of Jesus Christ Himself, which, as we know, has a triple dimension: it is the mission and office of Prophet, Priest and King. If we analyze carefully the conciliar texts, it is obvious that one should speak of a triple dimension of Christ's service and mission, rather than of three different functions. In fact, these functions are closely linked to one another, explain one another, condition one another and clarify one another. Consequently, it is from this threefold unity that our sharing in Christ's mission and office takes its origin. As Christians, members of the People of God, and subsequently as priests, sharers in the hierarchical order, we take our origin from the combination of the mission and office of our Teacher, who is Prophet, Priest and King, in order to witness to Him in a special way in the Church and before the world.

The priesthood in which we share through the sacrament of Orders, which has been for ever "imprinted" on our souls through a special sign from God, that is to say, the "character," *remains in explicit relationship with the common priesthood of the faithful*, that is to say, the priesthood of all the baptized, but at the same time it differs from that priesthood "essentially and not only in degree."[8] In this way the words of the author of the Letter to the Hebrews about the priest, who has been "chosen from among men...appointed to act on behalf of men,"[9] take on their full meaning.

At this point, it is better to reread once more the whole of this classical conciliar text, which expresses the basic truths on the theme of our vocation in the Church:

> "Christ the Lord, high priest taken from among men (cf. Heb. 5:1), made the new people 'a kingdom of priests to God, his Father' (Rv. 1:6, cf. 5:9-10). The baptized, by regeneration and the anointing of the Holy Spirit, are consecrated to be a spiritual house and a holy priesthood, that through all the works of Christian men they may offer spiritual sacrifices and proclaim the perfection of Him who has called them out of darkness into His marvelous light (cf. 1 Pt. 2:4-10). Therefore all the disciples of Christ, persevering in prayer and praising God together (cf. Acts 2:42-47), should present themselves as a sacrifice, living, holy and pleasing to God (cf. Rom. 12:1). They should everywhere on earth bear witness to Christ and give an answer to everyone who asks a reason for the hope of an eternal life which is theirs (cf. 1 Pt. 3:15).
>
> "Though they differ essentially and not only in degree, the common priesthood of the faithful and the ministerial or hierarchical priesthood are nonetheless ordered one to another; each in its own proper way

shares in the one priesthood of Christ. The ministerial priest, by the sacred power that he has, forms and rules the priestly people; in the person of Christ he effects the Eucharistic Sacrifice and offers it to God in the name of all the people. The faithful indeed, by virtue of their royal priesthood, participate in the offering of the Eucharist. They exercise that priesthood, too, by the reception of the sacraments, prayer and thanksgiving, the witness of a holy life, abnegation and active charity."[10]

The Priest as a Gift of Christ for the Community

4. We must consider down to the smallest detail not only the theoretical meaning but also the existential meaning of the mutual "relation" that exists between the hierarchical priesthood and the common priesthood of the faithful. The fact that they differ not only in degree but also in essence is a fruit of a particular aspect of the richness of the very priesthood of Christ, which is the one center and the one source, both of that participation which belongs to all the baptized and of that other participation which is reached through a distinct sacrament, which is precisely the sacrament of Orders. This sacrament, dear brothers, which is specific for us, which is the fruit of the special grace of vocation and the basis of our identity, by virtue of its very nature and of everything that it produces in our life and activity, serves to make the faithful aware of their common priesthood and to activate it[11]: the

sacrament reminds them that they are the People of God and enables them "to offer spiritual sacrifices,"[12] through which Christ Himself makes us an everlasting gift to the Father.[13] This takes place, above all, when the priest "by the sacred power that he has...in the person of Christ *(in persona Christi)* effects the Eucharistic Sacrifice and offers it to God in the name of all the people,"[14] as we read in the conciliar text quoted above.

Our sacramental priesthood, therefore, is a "hierarchical" and at the same time "ministerial" priesthood. It constitutes a special *ministerium*, that is to say, "service," in relation to the community of believers. It does not however take its origin from that community, as though it were the community that "called" or "delegated." The sacramental priesthood is truly a gift for this community and comes from Christ Himself, from the fullness of His priesthood. This fullness finds its expression in the fact that Christ, while making everyone capable of offering the spiritual sacrifice, calls some and enables them to be ministers of His own sacramental Sacrifice, the Eucharist—in the offering of which all the faithful share—in which are taken up all the spiritual sacrifices of the People of God.

Conscious of this reality, we understand how our priesthood is "hierarchical," that is to say, connected with the power of forming and governing the priestly people[15] and *precisely for this reason "ministerial."* We carry out this office, through which Christ Himself unceasingly "serves" the Father in the work of our salvation.

Our whole priestly existence is and must be deeply imbued with this service, if we wish to effect in an adequate way the Eucharistic Sacrifice *in persona Christi.*

The priesthood calls for a particular integrity of life and service, and precisely such integrity is supremely fitting for our priestly identity. In that identity there are expressed, at the same time, the greatness of our dignity and the "availability" proportionate to it: It is a question of the humble readiness to accept the gifts of the Holy Spirit and to transmit to others the fruits of love and peace, to give them that certainty of faith from which derive the profound understanding of the meaning of human existence and the capacity to introduce the moral order into the life of individuals and of the human setting.

Since the priesthood is given to us so that we can unceasingly serve others, after the example of Christ the Lord, the priesthood cannot be renounced because of the difficulties that we meet and the sacrifices asked of us. Like the Apostles, we have left everything to follow Christ[16]; therefore we must persevere beside Him also through the cross.

In the Service of the Good Shepherd

5. As I write, there pass before the eyes of my soul the vast and varied areas of human life, areas into which you are sent, dear brothers, like laborers into the Lord's vineyard.[17] But for you

there holds also the parable of the flock,[18] for, thanks to the priestly character, you share in the *pastoral charism*, which is a sign of a special relationship of *likeness to Christ, the Good Shepherd*. You are precisely marked with this quality in a very special way. Although care for the salvation of others is and must be a task of every member of the great community of the People of God, that is to say, also of all our brothers and sisters who make up the laity—as the Second Vatican Council so amply declared[19]—nevertheless, you priests are expected to have a care and commitment which are far greater and different from those of any lay person. And this is because your sharing in the priesthood of Jesus Christ differs from their sharing, "essentially and not only in degree."[20]

In fact, the priesthood of Jesus Christ is the first source and expression of an unceasing and ever effective care for our salvation, which enables us to look to Him precisely as the Good Shepherd. Do not the words "the good shepherd is one who lays down his life for his sheep"[21] refer to the sacrifice of the cross, to the definitive act of Christ's priesthood? Do they not show all of us that Christ the Lord, through the sacrament of Orders, has made us sharers in His priesthood, the road that we too must travel? Do these words not tell us that our vocation is a singular *solicitude for the salvation of our neighbor?* that this solicitude is a special *raison d'être* of our priestly life? that it is precisely this solicitude that gives it meaning, and that only through this solicitude can we find the full significance of our own life, perfection and holiness? This theme is taken up, at various places, in the conciliar Decree *Optatam totius*.[22]

However, this matter becomes more comprehensible in the light of the words of our same Teacher, who says: "For anyone who wants to save his life will lose it; but anyone who loses his life for my sake, and for the sake of the gospel, will save it."[23] These are mysterious words, and they seem like a paradox. But they cease to be mysterious if we try to put them into practice. Then the paradox disappears, and the profound simplicity of their meaning is fully revealed. May all of us be granted this grace in our priestly life and zealous service.

"The Supreme Art Is the Direction of Souls"[24]

6. The special care for the salvation of others, for truth, for the love and holiness of the whole People of God, for the spiritual unity of the Church—this care that has been entrusted to us by Christ, together with the priestly power, is exercised in various ways. Of course there is a difference in the ways in which you, dear brothers, fulfill your priestly vocation. Some in the ordinary pastoral work of parishes; others in mission lands; still others in the field of activities connected with the teaching, training and education of youth, or working in the various spheres and organizations whereby you assist in the development of social and cultural life; yet others near the suffering, the sick, the neglected, and sometimes, you yourselves bedridden and in

pain. These ways differ from one another, and it is just impossible to name them all one by one. They are necessarily numerous and different, because of the variety in the structure of human life, in social processes, and in the heritage and historical traditions of the various cultures and civilizations. Nevertheless, within all these differences, *you are always and everywhere the bearers of your particular vocation:* you are bearers of the grace of Christ, the eternal Priest, and bearers of the charism of the Good Shepherd. And this you can never forget; this you can never renounce; this you must put into practice at every moment, in every place and in every way. In this consists that "supreme art" to which Jesus Christ has called you. "The supreme art is the direction of souls," wrote St. Gregory the Great.

I say to you therefore, quoting these words of his: strive to be "artists" of pastoral work. There have been many such in the history of the Church. There speak to each of us, for example, St. Vincent de Paul, St. John of Avila, the holy Curé d'Ars, St. John Bosco, Blessed Maximilian Kolbe, and many, many others. Each of them was different from the others, was himself, was the son of his own time and was "up to date" with respect to his own time. But this "bringing up to date" of each of them was an original response to the Gospel, a response needed precisely for those times; it was the response of holiness and zeal. There is no other rule apart from this for "bringing ourselves up to date," in our priestly life and activity, with our time and with the world as it is today. Without any doubt, the various attempts and projects aimed at the "secularization" of the priestly life cannot be considered an adequate "bringing up to date."

Steward and Witness

7. The priestly life is built upon the foundation of the sacrament of Orders, which imprints on our soul the mark of an indelible character. This mark, impressed in the depths of our being, has its "personalistic" dynamism. *The priestly personality* must be *for others* a clear and plain *sign and indication.* This is the first condition for our pastoral service. The people from among whom we have been chosen and for whom we have been appointed [25] want above all to see in us such a sign and indication, and to this they have a right. It may sometimes seem to us that they do not want this, or that they wish us to be in every way "like them"; at times it even seems that they demand this of us. And here one very much needs a profound "sense of faith" and "the gift of discernment." In fact, it is very easy to let oneself be guided by appearances and fall victim to a fundamental illusion in what is essential. Those who call for the secularization of priestly life and applaud its various manifestations will undoubtedly abandon us when we succumb to temptation. We shall then cease to be necessary and popular. Our time is characterized by different forms of "manipulation" and "exploitation" of man, but we cannot give in to any of these.[26] In practical terms, the only priest who will always prove necessary to people is the priest who is

conscious of the full meaning of his priesthood: the priest who believes profoundly, who professes his faith with courage, who prays fervently, who teaches with deep conviction, who serves, who puts into practice in his own life the program of the beatitudes, who knows how to love disinterestedly, who is close to everyone, and especially to those who are most in need.

Our pastoral activity demands that we should be close to people and all their problems, whether these problems be personal, family or social ones, but it also demands that we should be close to all these problems "in a priestly way." Only then, in the sphere of all those problems, do we remain ourselves. Therefore, if we are really of assistance in those human problems, and they are sometimes very difficult ones, then we keep our identity and are really faithful to our vocation. With great perspicacity we must seek, together with all men, truth and justice, the true and definitive dimension of which we can only find in the Gospel, or rather in Christ Himself. Our task is to serve *truth and justice* in the dimensions of human "temporality," but *always in a perspective* that is the perspective *of eternal salvation*. This salvation takes into account the temporal achievements of the human spirit in the spheres of knowledge and morality, as the Second Vatican Council wonderfully recalled,[27] but it is not identical with them, and in fact it goes higher than them: "The things that no eye has seen and no ear has heard...all that God has prepared for those who love him."[28] Our brethren in the Faith, and unbelievers too, expect us always to be able to show them this perspective, to become real witnesses to it, to be dispensers of grace, to be servants of the Word of God. They expect us to be men of prayer.

Among us there are also those who have united their priestly vocation in a special way with an intense life of prayer and penance in the strictly contemplative form of their religious orders. Let them remember that their priestly ministry also in this form is—in a special way—"ordered" to the great solicitude of the Good Shepherd—solicitude for the salvation of every human being.

And this we must all remember: that it is not lawful for any of us to deserve the name of "hireling," that is to say, the name of one "to whom the sheep do not belong," one who, "since he is not the shepherd and the sheep do not belong to him, abandons the sheep and runs away as soon as he sees the wolf coming, and then the wolf attacks and scatters the sheep; this is because he is only a hired man and has no concern for the sheep."[29] The solicitude of every good shepherd is that all people "may have life and have it to the full,"[30] so that none of them may be lost,[31] but should have eternal life. Let us endeavor to make this solicitude penetrate deeply into our souls; let us strive to live it. May it characterize our personality, and be at the foundation of our priestly identity.

Meaning of Celibacy

8. Allow me at this point to touch upon the question of priestly celibacy. I shall deal with it

summarily, because it has already been considered in a profound and complete way during the Council, and subsequently in the Encyclical *Sacerdotalis caelibatus,* and again at the ordinary session of the 1971 Synod of Bishops. This reflection has shown itself to be necessary both in order to present the matter in a still more mature way, and also in order to explain even more deeply the meaning of the decision that the Latin Church took so many centuries ago and to which she has sought to be faithful, and desires to maintain this fidelity also in the future. The importance of the question under consideration is so great, and its link with the language of the Gospel itself so close, that in this case we cannot reason with categories different from those used by the Council, the Synod of Bishops and the great Pope Paul VI himself. We can only seek to understand this question more deeply and to respond to it more maturely, freeing ourselves from the various objections that have always—as happens today too—been raised against priestly celibacy, and also freeing ourselves from the different interpretations that appeal to criteria alien to the Gospel, to Tradition and to the Church's Magisterium—criteria, we would add, whose "anthropological" correctness and basis, in fact, are seen to be very dubious and of relative value.

Nor must we be too surprised at all the objections and criticisms which have intensified during the post-conciliar period, even though today in some places they seem to be growing less. Did not Jesus Christ, after He had presented the disciples with the question of the renunciation of marriage "for the sake of the kingdom of heaven," add these significant words: "Let anyone accept this who can"?[32] The Latin Church has wished, and continues to wish, referring to the example of Christ the Lord Himself, to the apostolic teaching and to the whole Tradition that is proper to her, that *all those who receive the sacrament of Orders should embrace this renunciation "for the sake of the kingdom of heaven."* This tradition, however, is linked with respect for different traditions of other Churches. In fact, this tradition constitutes a characteristic, a peculiarity and a heritage of the Latin Catholic Church, a tradition to which she owes much and in which she is resolved to persevere, in spite of all the difficulties to which such fidelity could be exposed, and also in spite of the various symptoms of weakness and crisis in individual priests. We are all aware that "we have this treasure in earthen vessels"[33]; yet we know very well that it is precisely a treasure.

Why is it a treasure? Do we wish thereby to reduce the value of marriage and the vocation to family life? Or are we succumbing to a Manichaean contempt for the human body and its functions? Do we wish in some way to devalue love, which leads a man and a woman to marriage and the wedded unity of the body, thus forming "one flesh"?[34] How could we think and reason like that, if we know, believe and proclaim, following St. Paul, that marriage is a "great mystery" in reference to Christ and the Church?[35] However, none of the reasons whereby people sometimes try to "convince us" of the inopportuneness of celibacy corresponds to the truth, the truth that the Church proclaims and seeks to realize in life through the commitment to which priests oblige themselves before ordination. The essential, proper and adequate reason, in fact, is contained in the truth that Christ declared when He spoke about the renunciation of marriage for the sake of the kingdom of heaven, and which St. Paul proclaimed when he wrote that each person in the Church has his or her own particular gifts.[36] Celibacy is precisely a "gift of the Spirit." A similar though different gift is contained in the vocation to true and faithful married love, directed towards procreation according to the flesh, in the very lofty context of the sacrament of Matrimony. It is obvious that this gift is fundamental for the building up of the great community of the Church, the People of God. But if this community wishes to respond fully to its vocation in Jesus Christ, there will also have to be realized in it, in the correct proportion, that other "gift," the gift of celibacy "for the sake of the kingdom of heaven."[37]

Why does the Latin Catholic Church link this gift not only with the life of those who accept the strict program of the evangelical counsels in religious institutes but also with the vocation to the hierarchical and ministerial priesthood? She does it because celibacy "for the sake of the kingdom" is not only an eschatological sign; it also has a great social meaning, in the present life, for the service of the People of God. Through his celibacy, the priest becomes the "man for others," in a different way from the man who, by binding himself in conjugal union with a woman, also becomes, as husband and father, a man "for others," especially in the radius of his own family: for his wife, and, together with her, for the children, to whom he gives life. The priest, by renouncing this fatherhood proper to married men, seeks another fatherhood and, as it were, even another motherhood, recalling the words of the Apostle about the children whom he begets in suffering.[38] These are children of his spirit, people entrusted to his solicitude by the Good Shepherd. These people are many, more numerous than an ordinary human family can embrace. The pastoral vocation of priests is great, and the Council teaches that it is universal: it is directed towards the whole Church,[39] and therefore it is of a missionary character. Normally, it is linked to the service of a particular community of the People of God, in which each individual expects attention, care and love. The heart of the priest, in order that it may be available for this service, must be free. Celibacy is a sign of a freedom that exists for the sake of service. According to this sign, the hierarchical or "ministerial" priesthood is, according to the tradition of our Church, more strictly "ordered" to the common priesthood of the faithful.

Test and Responsibility

9. The often widespread view that priestly celibacy in the Catholic Church is an institution imposed by law on those who receive the sacrament of Orders is the result of a misunderstanding, if not of downright bad faith. We all know

that it is not so. Every Christian who receives the sacrament of Orders commits himself to celibacy with full awareness and freedom, after a training lasting a number of years, and after profound reflection and assiduous prayer. He decides upon a life of celibacy only after he has reached a firm conviction that Christ is giving him this "gift" for the good of the Church and the service of others. Only then does he commit himself to observe celibacy for his entire life. It is obvious that such a decision obliges not only by virtue of a law laid down by the Church but also by virtue of personal responsibility. It is a matter here of *keeping one's word to Christ and the Church.* Keeping one's word is, at one and the same time, a duty and a proof of the priest's inner maturity; it is the expression of his personal dignity. It is shown in all its clarity when this keeping one's promise to Christ, made through a conscious and free commitment to celibacy for the whole of one's life, encounters difficulties, is put to the test, or is exposed to temptation—all things that do not spare the priest, any more than they spare any other Christian. At such a moment, the individual must seek support in more fervent prayer. Through prayer, he must find within himself that attitude of humility and sincerity before God and his own conscience; prayer is indeed the source of strength for sustaining what is wavering. Then it is that there is born a confidence like the confidence expressed by St. Paul in the words: "There is nothing that I cannot master with the help of the One who gives me strength."[40] These truths are confirmed by the experience of many priests and proved by the reality of life. The acceptance of these truths constitutes the basis of fidelity to the promise made to Christ and the Church, and that promise is at the same time the proof of genuine fidelity to oneself, one's own conscience, and one's own humanity and dignity. One must think of all these things especially at moments of crisis, and not have recourse to a dispensation, understood as an "administrative intervention," as though in fact it were not, on the contrary, a matter of a profound question of conscience and a test of humanity. God has a right to test each one of us in this way, since this earthly life is a time of testing for every human being. But God also wishes us all to emerge victorious from such tests, and He gives us adequate help for this.

Perhaps, not without good reason, one should add at this point that the commitment to married fidelity, which derives from the sacrament of Matrimony, creates similar obligations in its own sphere; this married commitment sometimes becomes a source of similar trials and experiences for husbands and wives, who also have a way of proving the value of their love in these "trials by fire." Love, in fact, in all its dimensions, is not only a call but also a duty. Finally, we should add that our brothers and sisters joined by the marriage bond *have the right to expect from us*, priests and pastors, good example and *the witness of fidelity to one's vocation until death,* a fidelity to the vocation that we choose through the sacrament of Orders just as they choose it through the sacrament of

Matrimony. Also in this sphere and in this sense we should understand our ministerial priesthood as "subordination" to the common priesthood of all the faithful, of the laity, especially of those who live in marriage and form a family. In this way, we serve in "building up the body of Christ"[41]; otherwise, instead of cooperating in the building up of that Body we weaken its spiritual structure. Closely linked to this building up of the Body of Christ is the authentic development of the human personality of each Christian —as also of each priest—a development that takes place according to the measure of the gift of Christ. The disorganization of the spiritual structure of the Church certainly does not favor the development of the human personality and does not constitute its proper testing.

Every Day We Have To Be Converted Anew

10. "What must we do, then?"[42]: dear brothers, this seems to be your question, just as the disciples and those who listened to Christ the Lord asked Him so often. What must the Church do, when it seems that there is a lack of priests, when their absence makes itself felt especially in certain countries and regions of the world? How are we to respond to the immense needs of evangelization, and how can we satisfy the hunger for the Word and the Body of the Lord? The Church, which commits herself to maintaining priestly celibacy as a particular gift for the kingdom of God, *professes faith in and expresses hope in* her Teacher, Redeemer and Spouse, and at the

same time in Him who is "Lord of the harvest" and "giver of the gift."[43] In fact, "every perfect gift is from above, coming down from the Father of lights."[44] We, for our part, cannot weaken this faith and confidence with our human doubting or our timidity.

In consequence, we must all be converted anew every day. We know that this is a fundamental exigency of the Gospel, addressed to everyone,[45] and all the more do we have to consider it as addressed to us. If we have the duty of helping others to be converted we have to do the same continuously in our own lives. Being converted means returning to the very grace of our vocation; it means meditating upon the infinite goodness and love of Christ, who has addressed each of us and, calling us by name, has said: "Follow me." Being converted means continually "giving an account" before the Lord of our hearts about our service, our zeal and our fidelity, for we are "Christ's servants, stewards entrusted with the mysteries of God."[46] Being converted also means "giving an account" of our negligences and sins, of our timidity, of our lack of faith and hope, of our thinking only "in a human way" and not "in a divine way." Let us recall, in this regard, the warning that Christ gave to Peter himself.[47] Being converted means, for us, seeking again the pardon and strength of God in the sacrament of Reconciliation, and thus always beginning anew, and every day progressing, overcoming ourselves, making spiritual conquests, giving cheerfully, for "God loves a cheerful giver."[48]

Being converted means "to pray continually and never lose heart."⁴⁹ *In a certain way prayer is the first and last condition for conversion,* spiritual progress and holiness. Perhaps in these recent years—at least in certain quarters—there has been too much discussion about the priesthood, the priest's "identity," the value of his presence in the modern world, etc., and on the other hand there has been too little praying. There has not been enough enthusiasm for actuating the priesthood itself through prayer, in order to make its authentic evangelical dynamism effective, in order to confirm the priestly identity. It is prayer that shows the essential style of the priest; without prayer this style becomes deformed. Prayer helps us always to find the light that has led us since the beginning of our priestly vocation, and which never ceases to lead us, even though it seems at times to disappear in the darkness. Prayer enables us to be converted continually, to remain in a state of continuous reaching out to God, which is essential if we wish to lead others to Him. Prayer helps us to believe, to hope and to love, even when our human weakness hinders us.

Prayer likewise enables us continually to rediscover the dimensions of that kingdom for whose coming we pray every day, when we repeat the words that Christ taught us. Then we realize *what our place is in the realization of the petition: "Thy kingdom come,"* and we see how necessary we are in its realization. And perhaps, when we pray, we shall see more easily those "fields...already white for harvest,"⁵⁰ and we shall understand the meaning of Christ's words as He looked at them: "So ask the Lord of the harvest to send laborers to his harvest."[51]

We must link prayer with continuous work upon ourselves: this is the *formatio permanens.* As is rightly pointed out by the Document on this theme issued by the Sacred Congregation for the Clergy,[52] this formation must be both interior, that is to say directed towards the deepening of the priest's spiritual life, and must also be pastoral and intellectual (philosophical and theological). Therefore, since our pastoral activity, the proclamation of the Word and the whole of the priestly ministry depend upon the intensity of our interior life, that activity must also find sustenance in assiduous study. It is not enough for us to stop at what we once learned in the seminary, even in cases where those studies were done at university level, which the Sacred Congregation for Catholic Education resolutely recommends. This process of intellectual formation must last all one's life, especially in modern times, which are marked—at least in many parts of the world—by the widespread development of education and culture. To the people who enjoy the benefits of this development we must be *witnesses* to Jesus Christ, and properly qualified ones. As teachers of truth and morality, we must tell them, convincingly and effectively, of the hope that gives us life.[53] And this also forms part of the process of daily conversion to love, through the truth.

Dear brothers: you who have borne "the burden of the day and the heat,"[54] who have put your hand to the plough and do not turn back,[55] and perhaps even more those of you who are doubtful of the meaning of your vocation or of the value of your service: think of the places where people anxiously await a priest, and where for many years, feeling the lack of such a priest, they do not cease to hope for his presence. And sometimes it happens that they meet in an abandoned shrine, and place on the altar a stole which they still keep, and recite all the prayers of the Eucharistic Liturgy; and then, at the moment that corresponds to the transubstantiation a deep silence comes down upon them, a silence sometimes broken by a sob...so ardently do they desire to hear the words that only the lips of a priest can efficaciously utter. So much do they desire Eucharistic Communion, in which they can share only through the ministry of a priest, just as they also so eagerly wait to hear the divine words of pardon: *Ego te absolvo a peccatis tuis!* So deeply do they feel the absence of a priest among them!... Such places are not lacking in the world. So if one of you doubts the meaning of his priesthood, if he thinks it is "socially" fruitless or useless, reflect on this!

We must be converted every day, we must rediscover every day the gift obtained from Christ Himself in the sacrament of Orders, by penetrating the importance of the salvific mission of the Church and by reflecting on the great meaning of our vocation in the light of that mission.

Mother of Priests

11. Dear brothers, at the beginning of my ministry I entrust all of you to the Mother of Christ, who in a special way is our Mother: the Mother of priests. In fact, the beloved disciple, who, as one of the Twelve, had heard in the Upper Room the words "Do this in memory of me,"[56] was given by Christ on the cross to His Mother, with the words: "Behold your son."[57] The man who on Holy Thursday received the power to celebrate the Eucharist was, by these words of the dying Redeemer, given to His Mother as her "son." All of us, therefore, who receive the same power through priestly ordination have in a certain sense a prior right to see her as our Mother. And so I desire that all of you, together with me, should find in Mary the Mother of the priesthood which we have received from Christ. I also desire that you should entrust your priesthood to her in a special way. Allow me to do it myself, *entrusting to the Mother of Christ* each one of you—without any exception—in a solemn and at the same time simple and humble way. And I ask each of you, dear brothers, to do it yourselves, in the way dictated to you by your own heart, especially by your love for Christ the Priest, and also by your own weakness, which goes hand in hand with your desire for service and holiness. I ask you to do this.

The Church of today speaks of herself especially in the Dogmatic Constitution *Lumen gentium*. Here too, in the last chapter, she proclaims that she looks to Mary as to the Mother of Christ, because she calls herself a mother and wishes to be a mother, begetting people for God to a new life.[58] Now, dear brothers: how near you are to this cause of God! How deeply it is imprinted upon your vocation, ministry and mission. In consequence, in the midst of the People of God that looks to Mary with immense love and hope, you must look to her with exceptional hope and love. Indeed, you must proclaim Christ who is her Son; and who will better communicate to you the truth about Him than His Mother? You must nourish human hearts with Christ: and who can make you more aware of what you are doing than she who nourished Him? "Hail, true Body, born of the Virgin Mary." In our "ministerial" priesthood there is *the wonderful and penetrating dimension of nearness to the Mother of Christ.* So let us try to live in that dimension. If I may be permitted to speak here of my own experience, I will say to you that in writing to you I am referring especially to my own personal experience.

As I communicate all this to you, at the beginning of my service to the universal Church, I do not cease to ask God to fill you, priests of Jesus Christ, with every blessing and grace, and as a token of this communion in prayer I bless you with all my heart, in the name of the Father and of the Son and of the Holy Spirit.

Accept this blessing. Accept the words of the new Successor of Peter, that Peter whom the Lord commanded: "And once you have recovered, you in your turn must strengthen your brothers."[59] Do not cease to pray for me together with the whole Church, so that I may respond to that exigency of a primacy of love that the Lord made the foundation of the mission of Peter, when He said to him: "Feed my lambs."[60] Amen.

From the Vatican, April 9, Passion Sunday (Palm Sunday), in the year 1979, the first of the Pontificate.

Pope John Paul II

FOOTNOTES

1. Cf. Mt. 20:12.
2. Cf. Jn. 21:15ff.
3. *Vobis enim sum episcopus, vobiscum sum Christianus: Serm.* 340, 1: *PL* 38, 1483.
4. Cf. I art. 15.
5. *Epistula ad Magnesios*, VI, 1: *Patres Apostolici* I, ed. Funk, p. 235.
6. Cf. Rom. 5:5; 1 Cor. 12:31; 13.
7. Heb. 5:1.
8. Dogmatic Constitution *Lumen gentium*, no. 10.
9. Heb. 5:1.
10. Dogmatic Constitution *Lumen gentium*, no. 10.
11. Cf. Eph. 4:11-12.
12. Cf. 1 Pt. 2:5.
13. Cf. 1 Pt. 3:18.
14. Dogmatic Constitution *Lumen gentium*, no. 10.
15. Cf. Dogmatic Constitution *Lumen gentium*, no. 10.
16. Cf. Mt. 19:27.
17. Cf. Mt. 20:1-16.
18. Cf. Jn. 10:1-16.
19. Cf. Dogmatic Constitution *Lumen gentium*, no. 11.
20. Dogmatic Constitution *Lumen gentium*, no. 10.
21. Jn. 10:11.
22. Cf. 8-11; 19-20.
23. Mk. 8:35.
24. St. Gregory the Great, *Regula pastoralis*, I, 1: *PL* 77, 14.
25. Cf. Heb. 5:1.
26. "Let us not deceive ourselves in thinking we serve the Gospel, if we try 'to dilute' our priestly charism...":

Pope John Paul II, *Discourse to the Clergy of Rome* (November 9, 1978), no. 3: *L'Osservatore Romano* (November 10, 1978), p. 2.

27. Cf. Pastoral Constitution *Gaudium et spes*, nos. 38-39, 42.

28. 1 Cor. 2:9.

29. Jn. 10:12-13.

30. Jn. 10:10.

31. Cf. Jn. 17:12.

32. Mt. 19:12.

33. Cf. 2 Cor. 4:7.

34. Gn. 2:24; cf. Mt. 19:6.

35. Cf. Eph. 5:32.

36. Cf. 1 Cor. 7:7.

37. Mt. 19:12.

38. Cf. 1 Cor. 4:15; Gal. 4:19.

39. Cf. Decree *Presbyterorum ordinis*, nos. 3, 6, 10, 12.

40. Phil. 4:13.

41. Eph. 4:12.

42. Lk. 3:10.

43. Mt. 9:38; cf. 1 Cor. 7:7.

44. James 1:17.

45. Cf. Mt. 4:17; Mk. 1:15.

46. 1 Cor. 4:1.

47. Cf. Mt. 16:23.

48. 2 Cor. 9:7.

49. Lk. 18:1.

50. Jn. 4:35.

51. Mt. 9:38.

52. Cf. Circular Letter of November 4, 1969: *AAS* 62 (1970), pp. 123ff.

53. Cf. 1 Pt. 3:15.

54. Mt. 20:12.

55. Cf. Lk. 9:62.

56. Lk. 22:19.

57. Jn. 19:26.

58. Cf. Dogmatic Constitution *Lumen gentium*, Chapter VIII.

59. Lk. 22:32.

60. Jn. 21:16.

Great Promise for the Future of Evangelization

After the Mass in Logan Circle, Philadelphia, on October 3, 1979, the Holy Father later went to Saint Charles Seminary to meet the priests, religious and seminarians of the archdiocese. He spoke to them as follows:

Beloved brothers and sons in Christ,

One of the things I wanted most to do during my visit to the United States has now arrived. I wanted to visit a seminary and meet the seminarians; and through you I would like to communicate to all seminarians how much you mean to me, and how much you mean for the future of the Church—for the future of the mission given to us by Christ.

You hold a special place in my thoughts and prayers. In your lives there is great promise for the future of evangelization. And you give us hope that the authentic renewal of the Church which was begun by the Second Vatican Council will be brought to fruition. But in order for this to happen, you must receive a solid and well-rounded preparation in the seminary. This personal conviction about the importance of seminaries prompted me to write these words in my Holy Thursday Letter to the Bishops of the Church: "The full reconstitution of the life of the seminaries throughout the Church will be the best proof of the achievement of the renewal to which the Council directed the Church."

1. If seminaries are to fulfill their mission in the Church, two activities in the overall program of the seminary are crucially important: the teaching of God's Word and discipline.

The intellectual formation of the priest, which is so vital for the times in which we live, embraces a number of the human sciences as well as the various sacred sciences. These all have an important place in your preparation for the priesthood. But the first priority for seminaries today is the teaching of God's Word in all its purity and integrity, with all its demands and in all its power. This was clearly affirmed by my beloved Predecessor Paul VI, when he stated that Sacred Scripture is "a perpetual source of spiritual life, the chief instrument for handing down Christian doctrine, and the center of all theological study" (Apostolic Constitution *Missale romanum*, April 3, 1969). Therefore if you, the seminarians of this generation, are to be adequately prepared to take on the heritage and challenge of the Second Vatican Council you will need to be well trained in the Word of God.

Secondly, the seminary must provide a sound discipline to prepare for a life of consecrated service in the image of Christ. Its purpose was well defined by the Second Vatican Council: "The discipline required by seminary life should not be regarded merely as a strong support of community life and of charity. For it is a necessary part of the whole training program designed to provide self-mastery, to foster solid maturity of personality, and to develop other traits of character which are extremely serviceable for the ordered and productive activity of the Church" *(Optatam totius,* 11).

When discipline is properly exercised, it can create an atmosphere of recollection which enables the seminarian to develop interiorly those attitudes which are so desirable in a priest, such as joyful obedience, generosity and self-sacrifice. In the different forms of community life that are appropriate for the seminary, you will learn the art of dialogue: the capacity to listen to others and to discover the richness of their personality, and the ability to give of yourself. Seminary discipline will reinforce, rather than diminish your freedom, for it will help develop in you those traits and attitudes of mind and heart which God has given you, and which enrich your humanity and help you to serve more effectively His people. Discipline will also assist you in ratifying day after day in your hearts the obedience you owe to Christ and His Church.

2. I want to remind you of the importance of fidelity. Before you can be ordained, you are called by Christ to make a free and irrevocable commitment to be faithful to Him and to His Church. Human dignity requires that you maintain this commitment, that you keep your promise to Christ no matter what difficulties you may encounter, and no matter what temptations you

may be exposed to. The seriousness of this irrevocable commitment places a special obligation upon the rector and faculty of the seminary—and in a particular way on the spiritual director—to help you to evaluate your own suitability for ordination. It is then the responsibility of the Bishop to judge whether you should be called to the priesthood.

It is important that one's commitment be made with full awareness and personal freedom. And so during these years in the seminary, take time to reflect on the serious obligations and the difficulties which are part of the priest's life. Consider whether Christ is calling you to the celibate life. You can make a responsible decision for celibacy only after you have reached the firm conviction that Christ is indeed offering you this gift, which is intended for the good of the Church and for the service of others (cf. Letter to Priests, no. 9).

To understand what it means to be faithful we must look to Christ, the "faithful witness" (Rev. 1:5), the Son who "learned to obey through what he suffered" (Heb. 5:8); to Jesus who said: "My aim is to do not my own will, but the will of him who sent me" (Jn. 5:30). We look to Jesus, not only to see and contemplate His fidelity to the Father despite all opposition (cf. Heb. 12:3), but also to learn from Him the means He employed in order to be faithful: especially prayer and abandonment to God's will (cf. Lk. 22:39ff.).

Remember that in the final analysis perseverance in fidelity is a proof, not of human strength and courage, but of the efficacy of Christ's grace. And so if we are going to persevere we shall have to be men of prayer who, through the Eucharist, the Liturgy of the Hours and our personal encounters with Christ, find the courage and grace to be faithful. Let us be confident then, remembering the words of St. Paul: "There is nothing that I cannot master with the help of the one who gives me strength" (Phil. 4:13).

3. My brothers and sons in Christ, keep in mind the priorities of the priesthood to which you aspire: namely, prayer and the ministry of the Word (Acts 6:4).

"It is prayer that shows the essential style of the priest; without prayer this style becomes deformed. Prayer helps us always to find the light that has led us since the beginning of our priestly vocation, and which never ceases to lead us.... Prayer enables us to be converted continually, to remain in a state of continuous reaching out to God, which is essential if we wish to lead others to Him. Prayer helps us to believe, to hope and to love..." (Letter to Priests, no. 10).

It is my hope that during your years in the seminary you will develop an ever greater hunger for the Word of God (cf. Amos 8:11). Meditate on this Word daily and study it continually, so that your whole life may become a proclamation of Christ, the Word made flesh (cf. Jn. 1:14). In this Word of God are the beginning and end of all ministry, the purpose of all pastoral activity, the rejuvenating source for faithful perseverance and the one thing which can give meaning and unity to the varied activities of a priest.

4. "Let the message of Christ, in all its richness, find a home with you" (Col. 3:16). In the knowledge of Christ you have the key to the Gospel. In the knowledge of Christ you have an understanding of the needs of the world. Since He became one with us in all things but sin, your union with Jesus of Nazareth could never, and will never be an obstacle to understanding and responding to the needs of the world. And finally, in the knowledge of Christ, you will not only discover and come to understand the limitations of human wisdom and of human solutions to the needs of humanity, but you will also experience the power of Jesus, and the value of human reason and human endeavor when they are taken up in the strength of Jesus, when they are redeemed in Christ.

May our Blessed Mother Mary protect you today and always.

5. May I also take this opportunity to greet the lay people who are present today at Saint Charles Seminary. Your presence here is a sign of your esteem for the ministerial priesthood, as well as being a reminder of that close cooperation between laity and priests which is needed if the mission of Christ is to be fulfilled in our time. I am happy that you are present and I am grateful for all that you do for the Church in Philadelphia.

In particular I ask you to pray for these young men, and for all seminarians, that they may persevere in their calling. Please pray for all priests and for the success of their ministry among God's people. And please pray the Lord of the harvest to send more laborers into His vineyard, the Church.

A Deep Commitment to Authentic Christian Living

On October 7, 1979, Pope John Paul II met professors and theologians of the Catholic University of America. He addressed them as follows.

Dear brothers and sisters in Christ,

1. Our meeting today gives me great pleasure, and I thank you sincerely for your cordial welcome. My own association with the university world, and more particularly with the Pontifical Theological Faculty of Krákow, makes our encounter all the more gratifying for me. I cannot but feel at home with you. The sincere expressions with which the chancellor and the president of the Catholic University of America have confirmed, in the name of all of you, the faithful adherence to Christ and the generous commitment to the service of truth and charity of your Catholic associations and institutions of higher learning are appreciated.

Ninety-one years ago, Cardinal Gibbons and the American bishops requested the foundation of the Catholic University of America, as a university "destined to provide the Church with worthy ministers for the salvation of souls and the propagation of religion and to give the republic most worthy citizens." It seems appropriate to me on this occasion to address myself not only to this great institution, so irrevocably linked to the bishops of the United States who have founded it and who generously support it, but also to all the Catholic universities, colleges, and academies of post-secondary learning in your land, those with formal and sometimes juridical links with the Holy See, as well as all those who are "Catholic."

2. Before doing so, though, allow me first to mention the ecclesiastical faculties, three of which are established here at the Catholic University of America. I greet these faculties and all who dedicate their best talents in them. I offer my prayers for the prosperous development and the unfailing fidelity and success of these faculties. In the Apostolic Constitution *Sapientia Christiana*, I have dealt directly with these institutions in order to provide guidance and to ensure that they fulfill their role in meeting the needs of the Christian community in today's rapidly changing circumstances.

I also wish to address a word of praise and admiration for the men and women, especially priests and religious, who dedicate themselves to all forms of campus ministry. Their sacrifices and efforts to bring the true message of Christ to the university world, whether secular or Catholic, cannot go unnoticed.

The Church also greatly appreciates the work and witness of those of her sons and daughters whose vocation places them in non-Catholic universities in your country. I am sure that their Christian hope and Catholic patrimony bring an enriching and irreplaceable dimension to the world of higher studies.

A special word of gratitude and appreciation also goes to the parents and students who, sometimes at the price of great personal and financial sacrifice, look toward the Catholic universities and colleges for the training that unites faith and science, culture and the Gospel values.

To all engaged in administration, teaching or study in Catholic colleges and universities I would apply the words of Daniel: "They who are learned shall shine like the brightness of the firmament; and those that instruct many in justice, as stars for all eternity" (Dn. 12:3). Sacrifice and generosity have accomplished heroic results in the foundation and development of these institutions. Despite immense financial strain, enrollment problems, and other obstacles, divine Providence and the commitment of the whole People of God have allowed us to see these Catholic institutions flourish and advance.

3. I would repeat here before you what I told the professors and students of the Catholic universities in Mexico when I indicated three aims that are to be pursued. A Catholic university or college must make a specific contribution to the Church and to society through high quality scientific research, in-depth study of prob-

lems, and a just sense of history, together with the concern to show the full meaning of the human person regenerated in Christ, thus favoring the complete development of the person. Furthermore, the Catholic university or college must train young men and women of outstanding knowledge who, having made a personal synthesis between faith and culture, will be both capable and willing to assume tasks in the service of the community and of society in general, and to bear witness to their Faith before the world. And finally, to be what it ought to be, a Catholic college or university must set up, among its faculty and students, a real community which bears witness to a living and operative Christianity, a community where sincere commitment to scientific research and study goes together with a deep commitment to authentic Christian living.

This is your identity. This is your vocation. Every university or college is qualified by a specific mode of being. Yours is the qualification of being Catholic, of affirming God, His revelation and the Catholic Church as the guardian and interpreter of that revelation. The term "Catholic" will never be a mere label, either added or dropped according to the pressures of varying factors.

4. As one who for long years has been a university professor, I will never tire of insisting on the eminent role of the university, which is to instruct but also to be a place of scientific research. In both these fields, its activity is closely related to the deepest and noblest aspira-

tion of the human person: the desire to come to the knowledge of truth. No university can deserve the rightful esteem of the world of learning unless it applies the highest standards of scientific research, constantly updating its methods and working instruments, and unless it excels in seriousness, and therefore, in freedom of investigation. Truth and science are not gratuitous conquests, but the result of a surrender to objectivity and of the exploration of all aspects of nature and man. Whenever man himself becomes the object of investigation, no single method, or combination of methods, can fail to take into account, beyond any purely natural approach, the full nature of man. Because he is bound by the total truth about man, the Christian will, in his research and in his teaching, reject any partial vision of human reality, but he will let himself be enlightened by his faith in the creation of God and the redemption of Christ.

The relationship to truth explains, therefore, the historical bond between the university and the Church. Because she herself finds her origin and her growth in the words of Christ, which are the liberating truth (cf. Jn. 8:32), the Church has always tried to stand by the institutions that serve, and cannot but serve, the knowledge of truth. The Church can rightfully boast of being in a sense the mother of universities. The names of Bologna, Padua, Prague and Paris shine in the earliest history of intellectual endeavor and human progress. The continuity of the historic tradition in this field has come down to our day.

5. An undiminished dedication to intellectual honesty and academic excellence are seen, in a Catholic university, in the perspective of the Church's mission of evangelization and service. This is why the Church asks these institutions, your institutions, to set out, without equivocation, your Catholic nature. This is what I have desired to emphasize in my Apostolic Constitution *Sapientia Christiana*, where I stated: "Indeed, the Church's mission of spreading the Gospel not only demands that the Good News be preached ever more widely and to ever greater numbers of men and women, but that the very power of the Gospel should permeate thought patterns, standards of judgment, and the norms of behavior; in a word, it is necessary that the whole of human culture be steeped in the Gospel. The cultural atmosphere in which a human being lives has a great influence upon his or her way of thinking and, thus, of acting. Therefore, a division between faith and culture is more than a small impediment to evangelization, while a culture penetrated with the Christian spirit is an instrument that favors the spreading of the Good News" *(Sapientia Christiana,* I). The goals of Catholic higher education go beyond education for production, professional competence, technological and scientific competence; they aim at the ultimate destiny of the human person, at the full justice and holiness born of truth (cf. Eph. 4:24).

6. If then your universities and colleges are institutionally committed to the Christian message, and if they are part of the Catholic com-

munity of evangelization, it follows that they have an essential relationship to the hierarchy of the Church. And here I want to say a special word of gratitude, encouragement and guidance for the theologians. The Church needs her theologians, particularly in this time and age so profoundly marked by deep changes in all areas of life and society. The bishops of the Church, to whom the Lord has entrusted the keeping of the unity of the Faith and the preaching of the message—individual bishops for their dioceses; and bishops collegially, with the Successor of Peter for the universal Church—we all need your work, your dedication and the fruits of your reflection. We desire to listen to you, and we are eager to receive the valued assistance of your responsible scholarship.

But true theological scholarship, and by the same token, theological teaching, cannot exist and be fruitful without seeking its inspiration and its source in the Word of God as contained in Sacred Scripture and in the Sacred Tradition of the Church, as interpreted by the authentic Magisterium throughout history (cf. *Dei Verbum*, no. 10). True academic freedom must be seen in relation to the finality of the academic enterprise, which looks to the total truth of the human person. The theologian's contribution will be enriching for the Church only if it takes into account the proper function of the bishops and the rights of the faithful. It devolves upon the bishops of the Church to safeguard the Christian authenticity and unity of faith and moral teaching, in accordance with the injunction of the Apostle Paul: "Proclaim the message and, welcome or unwelcome, insist on it. Refute falsehood, correct error, call to obedience..." (2 Tm. 4:2). It is the right of the faithful not to be troubled by theories and hypotheses that they are not expert in judging, or that are easily simplified or manipulated by public opinion for ends that are alien to the truth. On the day of his death, John Paul I stated: "Among the rights of the faithful, one of the greatest is the right to receive God's Word in all its entirety and purity..." (September 28, 1978). It behooves the theologian to be free, but with the freedom that is openness to the truth and the light that comes from faith and from fidelity to the Church.

In concluding I express to you once more my joy in being with you today. I remain very close to your work and your concerns. May the Holy Spirit guide you. May the intercession of Mary, Seat of Wisdom, sustain you always in your irreplaceable service of humanity and the Church. God bless you.

Theology Dynamically Involved in the Prophetic Mission of the Church

During his visit to the Pontifical Gregorian University on December 15, 1979, the Holy Father delivered the following address.

Venerable brothers and dearest sons and daughters:

1. Tonight I am in your midst with a deep sense of joy for this solemn, yet homely meeting which officially allows me to meet the teaching staff of this illustrious center of ecclesiastical studies, the students who receive their intellectual formation here, as well as both its officials and workers whose competence keeps it running smoothly.

I willingly accepted the invitation your authorities made a while ago, not only because I recognize it as a praiseworthy sign of devotion and fidelity to the Successor of St. Peter, but also because it affords me the opportunity, in this the fiftieth anniversary of your being in your new campus at Piazza della Pilotta, to make a concrete gesture of the esteem in which I hold this University and its sister institutes.

So I greet with fraternal affection Their Eminences, Cardinal Gabriel M. Garrone, the Chancellor; the former Rector of this Atheneum, Pablo Muñoz Vega; the Superior General of the Society of Jesus and Vice Chancellor of the University, Father Pedro Arrupe; the Rector, Father Carlo Martini; and its distinguished professors, some of whom I have the pleasure of knowing personally, while others I have been able to meet and appreciate through their published books and articles.

I greet you with deepest feelings, dear young people who have come to this *Alma Mater* from every part of the world, impelled by the desire to enrich your minds with treasures of Catholic doctrine and to strengthen your hearts through a prolonged stay in the places made holy by the blood of the Apostles and martyrs and made illustrious by the remarkable monuments of the traditions glorious in both the Christian and humanistic realms.

I would also like to greet in a particularly warm way the rector, the professors and students of the Pontifical Institute of Oriental Studies whose function in the Church has played no small part in recent developments in ecumenical dialogue, and of the Pontifical Biblical Institute which celebrates the seventieth anniversary of its foundation in the happy awareness of both having rendered and continuing to render an important service to the Church in performing the duty set for it according to the Apostolic Letter *Vinea electa* of Pope St. Pius X in far off 1909, on May 7.

In the meantime the Biblicum has truly become a "center of higher studies for Holy Writ," able to promote "in a proper way the doctrine of the Bible and all the studies which attend it in a way which is more efficacious and follows the sense of the Catholic Church," according to the express wishes of the Holy Pontiff (cf. *AAS* 1, 1909, pp. 447f.). In these decades very many students have "trained and perfected themselves" there, submitting to the disciplines necessary to develop the study of the Word of God done "so that what is accomplished both in public and in private, in writing or teaching..., be performed with due seriousness and with wholesome doctrine" *(ibid.,* p. 448). Further, if one adds up the large and distinguished series of scientific publications "published in the name and with the authority of the institute" (cf. *ibid.,* p. 448) in the course of these seventy years, one should not be surprised that the Biblicum is held in such high esteem in the world of scientific scholarship throughout the world. The Pope is happy to say "well done!" to your administrators and professors on this anniversary.

2. My very presence in your midst, dear members of the Pontifical Gregorian University, expresses and bears witness to the interest with which I follow your activities, and of the trust I place in your work; also of the hope with which I await the fruits of your toil, from which the Church ought to benefit greatly.

In fact, the Christian community awaits a sound contribution from you: that reasoned and systematic reflection on the Faith which is the specific function of theology. Moreover, this has been the task which has qualified the "Roman College" practically from its inception, more than four centuries ago, when it was begun providentially through the apostolic zeal of Saint Ignatius of Loyola and then gradually developed until it reached the imposing dimensions of the present University with its variety of faculties and specializations.

What a noble line of professors, often at the highest level, has brought honor to your institution over the many years of its history! Their constant desire has been to pore over the depths of the revealed Word of God and the Church's living tradition with understanding and love. And I am pleased to emphasize as a legitimate cause of pride for your University that they did all this, engaging in the twofold work which is of fundamental importance to every piece of theological research. Firstly and above all, they had a constant openness which bespoke loyalty and docility to the directions of the Magisterium; and this harmonizes with the spirit proper to the Society of Jesus which animates this center of learning. And, secondly, they have always been open to scientific advancements which have import for theology.

This last point deserves to be dwelt on a little. In effect, the history of your University shows that here theology was never seen as an isolated discipline. It has always been connected with other disciplines, as it was designed in the old *Ratio Studiorum* which proposed to assume the integration of research and theological knowledge in a way in which one's knowledge was thus stamped with modernity. In this way one tends towards a construct which is "Christian Wisdom." The recent Apostolic Constitution on the universities and ecclesiastical faculties describes this as a reality which stimulates one "to gather events and human activities into a single living synthesis together with religious values, under whose guidance all things are coordinated one with the other for the glory of God and the holistic development of humankind; which development embraces the goods of both body and spirit" (Apostolic Constitution *Sapientia Christiana*, Foreword, I).

3. There is a point here on which I would like to dwell. In its millenial history, theology has always sought out "allies" which would aid it in penetrating all the riches of the divine plan as it reveals itself in human history and as one reflects on the magnificence of the cosmos. These "allies" have shown up in the sciences and other academic disciplines, which have continued to emerge under the impulse of a desire to know more deeply the mystery of humankind and its history and the ambience of human life.

The heads of the Roman College showed an awareness of this from its very beginning. It amazes one who examines the story of this center of learning to see how, alongside theology, not only philosophy and literature, but also arts, archaeology and the study of the heritage and cultures of ancient times were studied, as well as the physical sciences, mathematics, astronomy and astrophysics. Evidently they sensed a need to be in close contact with all the studies which, with the passage of the years, made up the changing vision which man had of himself and of the world which surrounded him. And if one would only realize that students of that time were conditioned by their cultural ambience, one could accept that there were brilliant forerunners and freer spirits, like St. Robert Bellarmine in the case of Galileo Galilei, who wished to avoid useless tensions and harmful rigidities between faith and science.

The natural sciences treated in those days have become ever more specialized, and many have gone beyond the scope of work proper to an ecclesiastical university. However, the fundamental urge to take into account all the progress made by science in things pertaining to man and the context of his life still remains a valid one for us. To be precise, in view of this, it is still desirable to have a rapport between an ecclesiastical university and state universities, together with the research centers run in a modern society. In fact, "the gap between faith and culture constitutes an impediment to evangelization, while, on the contrary, a culture in which the Christian spirit breathes life is a valid instrument for the diffusion of the Gospel" (Apostolic Constitution *Sapientia Christiana*, Foreword, I).

4. From the institutional and organizational point of view, your university has provided strong "allies" for theology by the creation of a series of chairs in the emerging disciplines, which have developed into institutes and facul-

ties absorbed into the university juridically. They exist at the side of theology, and of these the oldest—as old as the faculty of theology itself—is that of philosophy.

I would like to say something specific at this point on philosophical studies in general, to which I am linked by long experience of teaching and research. In an ecclesiastical university, it is important that philosophy fulfill its traditional mandate, which is the methodical investigation of the problems native to it and the search for their solution based on our ever valid philosophical patrimony, using the light of reason as its guide (cf. Apostolic Constitution *Sapientia Christiana,* Special Norms, art. 79, par. 1).

But it is also important to notice that the relationship to our past patrimony ought not to be construed as a foreclosure of the possibility of a study which would endow modern and contemporary currents with value. What I said at the beginning of my pastoral ministry on the Chair of Peter was a cry to all not to fear to throw open the doors to Christ and bears repetition with regard to the great movements of contemporary thought, endowing with value their capacity for and inclination towards the whole truth.

There is no time now to rehearse the list of faculties, recalling the time of their institution. I cannot do more than note that at the institution of each there was an awareness on the part of the officials of the university of an increasing differentiation in the field of religious studies and the necessity of a constant focus on the most recent research on humankind. Each faculty and institute represents a new stage in the development of the ecclesiastical sciences which surround theology.

5. Tonight, my dear friends, I am happy to encourage you to follow this way. You will do it, obviously, with the prudence and discernment which should attend the enterprise. In fact, theology ought to choose its "allies" according to the criteria supplied by its own methodology. There are currents of thought which, either because of their foundations or because of the developments made of them by their promoters, do not offer the requisites necessary for a useful collaboration with theological research. In such a case it will be indispensable to offer clear proofs, arrived at critically, in evaluating the contributions offered by one or the other philosophical or scientific system, and to choose what will prove useful in advancing theological knowledge and to reject what impedes that advance. The instruction of St. Paul has its point here: "Test everything, hold on to what is good" (1 Thes. 5:21).

In fact, there are perspectives, points of view and philosophical languages decidedly lacking in usefulness. There are scientific systems so poor or so closed as to render any translation and interpretation of the Word of God impossible. To take on these systems as allies in an acritical way would mean theological suicide and cause irreparable damage. The story of some theological trends which have gone astray in the past decades is instructive.

Therefore it is necessary to cultivate in yourselves the capacity "to discern." This calls for a solid theological formation by virtue of which the student who has mastered a method and controls the instruments of theological research can probe the richness hidden in the Word of God. So this tool will become in his hands "sharper than any two-edged blade," able to "penetrate up to the point where soul separates from spirit, bones from marrow, and to search the feelings and thoughts of the heart" (Heb. 4:12).

If one presupposes this firm base, the meeting with the other disciplines will prove truly fruitful, fostering a creative exchange without risking a hybrid mixture or dangerous distortions. Thus, to use the language of St. Paul, one will not find oneself in the situation of "children tossed about on every wave, borne here and there by every wind of doctrine, according to the deceits of men, with which tricks they wish to lead one into error" (Eph. 4:14).

6. In speaking of the openness theology ought to cultivate in relation to the other disciplines, it comes to me immediately to recall another openness which is even more essential: the openness to the concrete problems of human beings, the openness which is in the service of the ecclesial community.

Theology is an ecclesial science because it grows in the Church and works on the Church. Therefore theology is never the private affair of a specialist, cut off in a kind of ivory tower. It is a service of the Church and therefore ought to feel itself dynamically involved in the mission of the Church, particularly in its prophetic mission.

It is not that theology ought to be a substitute for preaching, but by deepening and extending one's knowledge of Revelation, theology is an important aid to the ecclesial office of preaching and, in a certain way, becomes the base for our liturgical and pastoral activity.

Dear friends, this pastoral aspect ought to stand in the forefront of your work in the University and ought not to deter you from its seriousness, but rather should be a stimulus for generosity in your work in view of the relevance which your hard work has in bringing to life the salvific plan of God. Theological thought and pastoral action are not at loggerheads with each other; rather they foster one another. Scientific investigation and evangelization go together; the one bears and sustains the other.

My dear friends, we ought to serve the men and women of our time. We ought to serve them in their thirst for total truth, evolved in them by Christ the Redeemer of humankind: a thirst for human rights and justice, for morality and spirituality; a thirst for ultimate and definitive truths; a thirst for the Word of God; a thirst for unity among Christians.

Mark it well, dear professors and students, and also your co-workers here in the University: the realities which you come here to probe, the pedagogic and formative service which you render here, the doctrines which you disseminate from here, are not something peripheral, as if they were luxuries over against the real problems of our world. Rather, they touch on the most profound aspects of existence which Christ Himself came to illumine with His life, death and resurrection. They are the realities which all men and women of our time need in order to open themselves to love and hope. Humanity could not survive without this love, without this hope.

7. I have referred to the pedagogic and formative function of the University. This leads me to turn to you men and women from all over the world who study here. I deeply feel your presence as a force for life in the Church and I detect in you, as I wrote in the Encyclical *Redemptor hominis*, the desire to "come closer to Christ and to 'appropriate' and assimilate all the reality of the Incarnation and redemption in order to find yourselves" (cf. no. 10). And I confirm here the conviction that if you satisfy this desire and activate this deep process, then each one of you "will bear fruit not only of adoration of God, but also of deep wonder at himself" and there will be born in each "that deep amazement at man's worth and dignity, which is the Gospel, or better, the Good News" (cf. *ibid.*, no. 10).

To this end it is necessary that each of you become an active part of the thought process which goes on in a university so that this "deep wonder" mature in you in your reasoned reflection and your scientifically validated conclusions. Therefore, I wish to stimulate an active, full and joyous participation in all of you as you penetrate the revealed mystery and the realities connected with it. You must be engaged in it yourselves in order to collaborate responsibly in the cognitive process. You are not mere assimilators of ideas; you are researchers called to bring about your own contribution to the progress of theological knowledge; all this not only under the direction of your professors, but together with them.

Therefore, it is important that you not limit yourselves to study; you must, above all, master a method which shapes the way you conduct your study, so as to be able to follow the road by yourselves and at your own pace. Academic degrees are really only official recognition of scientific maturity already acquired. Besides, it is obvious that one's theological reflections will have pastoral import because of this maturity. It makes you able to enter into dialogue almost at once with the mentality, the desires, the expectations and the language of men and women of our time.

It is evident that such an active participation in the cognitive process which happens in the university ought to be fulfilled gradually. It should adapt itself to the nature of the cycles on which your curriculum of study is based. The first cycle, in fact, is designed to provide general information through a well modulated exposition of all the prime disciplines; this, together with an introduction into the use of a scientific method. In the cycles which follow, however, one embarks on the study of a particular segment of the disciplines at the same time as one is introduced to a more complicated experience of doing scientific research according to a method. This takes one gradually to a level of scientific maturity (cf. Apostolic Constitution *Sapientia Christiana*, General Norms, art. 40).

Here it is important that I recall something which ought to be one of the chief characteristics of a university: namely, the necessity to "fulfill one's teaching office especially in the institutional cycle where, above all, those doctrines should be communicated which deal with the patrimony of the Church" (*ibid.*, Special Norms, art. 70). In fact, it is only on the basis of a responsible assimilation of such a patrimony that one can stimulate creativity and the spirit of research among one's students done in a union of minds and aims and given support by its very movement towards the one truth.

In this way one will bring about a great cognitive drive in which all will faithfully contribute. This includes the university whole and entire, employing all its components in the penetration of revealed truth and employing all the methods of research.

8. Who does not see the fundamental importance which this cognitive drive has for the Church's life and, in particular, for its unity? Furthermore, St. Ignatius was thinking of this when he founded the Roman College. He conceived of it as "a university for all peoples" which was to be sited in Rome close to the Vicar of Christ and linked to him firmly with fidelity; and it was to be a service for the churches from around the world which would foster a preaching of the Gospel which was instinct with both accuracy and a lively sense of Catholic unity, and all this in the midst of a profound theological

reflection on the faith. In this way he made a noteworthy contribution toward maintaining the unity of the Christian world derived from the depths of his vision of it.

Since its inception, students and professors of different nations and cultures have lived and collaborated in harmony within the structures of this center of learning as they learned to know one another, mutually, and mature on a foundation of a commonly held faith, which is the permanent bond of unity. It is this Catholic unity which has been vigorously proclaimed throughout the whole world through the doctrine, life and frequent martyrdoms of your alumni, of whom nineteen have been canonized and twenty-four beatified by the Church. This same Catholic unity has been served by sixteen Popes, innumerable cardinals, bishops, priests and—for some time now in ever increasing numbers—religious women and lay people. All of these have deepened their faith in the lecture halls of this university.

In the light of such a noble tradition, I say to all you who hear me: A great mission awaits you in the service of all the Churches. Here you are learning to value yourselves and to be brothers and sisters in a common work and in a disciplined search for unique truth. The knowledge which you acquire here, and the experiences you have, you will put at the service of the Churches of the whole world. In fact it is necessary that each local Church develop its peculiar strengths of expression and exploit its own religious and cultural traditions. But to do this it is equally as necessary that you face among yourselves, weigh and exchange such experiences in an atmosphere of common understanding and mutual openness so that the communion of minds and hearts might be preserved.

This is the most important function of a center which is a "university for all peoples" in the heart of Rome and close to the Pope. In making use of the age-old tradition of collaboration at the level both of students and of teachers, among peoples of different cultures, languages and mentalities, this can and should contribute to the maintenance and growth of a sense of fraternity, to mutual sensitivity and to the ability to understand oneself, without which one can neither safeguard unity nor tend towards having it.

The Pope counts on you to follow in this tradition of service for unity. When you men and women return to your Churches, you ought to take on various responsibilities of ministry and service. You know how to keep alive amidst all these responsibilities and amidst your many contacts this sense of catholicity and openness to all people and things, which is as the very lifebreath of the Church. You are the promotors of unity and brotherhood, upholding openness and dialogue between the diverse languages and cultures. Make your own contribution to the harmonious fusion of every culture's individual characteristics with all those elements which are the permanent fonts of Catholic unity.

9. And I encourage you professors and offer my grateful acknowledgment of the fact that you labor in a situation which demands a partic-

ular sacrifice and a constant focusing of your attention and openness to whatever comes from not only every part of the Catholic world but also from the entire human family.

I want you to do your work for truth courageously and openly, free of every prejudice and pinching narrowness of mind. Fix your gaze on our central mystery which is the Christ who is at work and reveals Himself in His Church and has wished to place in the Church of Rome the visible sign of the unity of His body, entrusting to Peter and his Successors the work of guaranteeing the integral proclamation of Catholic truth at the service of the Church and of the whole human race.

With your study let your love for Christ grow so that your teaching can convey to the young a living experience of Him. Do not forget that the fundamental scope of your work is the formation of Christians, and in particular of priests, capable of making in the future a real contribution of pastoral activity by the witness of their word but above all by their lives.

My dear professors, the Pope has also been a man dedicated to the life of study in the university, and he understands the difficulties of your work very well. He understands the irksome weight of the task and the sharpness of the obstacles to your work and your ideals. Do not give way to discouragement brought on by the day's tensions. Realize that each day is to be creative; and do not content yourselves too easily with what was useful in the past. Have the courage to explore new ways, but be prudent about it. The Apostolic Constitution *Sapientia Christiana* recognizes that there is "a real freedom to do research and to teach, in order that one can grow in one's knowledge and comprehension of divine truth" (General Norms, art. 39, and 1, 1).

Especially to bring this about it is necessary that you have an interior balance, strength of mind and spirit and, above all, a profound humility of heart which will make you disciples attentive to the truth and docile hearers of God's Word which is authentically interpreted by the Magisterium. St. Thomas warns us that the proud "cannot stomach the excellence of truth, but delight in their own excellence" *(S. Theol.,* II-II, q. 162, a. 3, ad 1).

10. My dear professors, students and co-workers, Providence has made this meeting the sweeter by the nearness of the feast of the Nativity. Within a few days we will relive the ineffable mystery of the birth of the eternal Word of God in time. For one who is searching, God has given Himself the features, the voice, the gestures of a human being. The invisible God has become, in Christ, Emmanuel, God with us.

The words of the Christmas preface come to mind: "In the mystery of the Word Incarnate a new light of your glory has appeared to the eyes of our mind, because by knowing God in a visible way we are seized with a love of invisible realities." Do we not find the deep meaning of your work in the University synthesized in these words? Christ is the true "method" of every theological research because He is "the Way"

(Jn. 14:6) through which God has come to us and through whom we can reach God. He it is who sustains your studies. He is the center of your life and of your prayer. Follow this "Way" with enthusiasm, sustained by faith and love!

In calling down on you and your work an abundance of celestial light, I place your University and its allied institutes under the watchful protection of her who is the Mother of Wisdom, because she is the Mother of Christ. May Mary be at your side as you do your daily work.

I offer you my apostolic blessing with my most cordial wishes for a joyful and holy Christmas.

Your Lives Offer Promise for the Church's Future

On February 22, 1980, Pope John Paul went to the Pontifical North American College on the Janiculum Hill, and during the concelebrated Mass His Holiness delivered the following homily.

"You are the Messiah," Simon Peter answered, "the Son of the living God!" (Mt. 16:16)

These words of personal faith and divine inspiration mark the beginning of Peter's mission in the history of the People of God. These words also mark the beginning of a new era in the history of salvation. From the moment these words were spoken at Caesarea Philippi, the history of the People of God was linked to the man who had pronounced them: "You are Peter and on this rock I will build my church" (Mt. 16:18).

These words have a special meaning for me. They express what is the heart of my mission as the Successor of Peter at the end of the twentieth century. Jesus Christ is the center of the universe and of history. He alone is the Redeemer of every human being. In God's inscrutable Providence I have been chosen to continue the mission of Peter and to repeat with similar conviction: "You are the Messiah—the Christ—the Son of the living God." Nothing in my life and ministry can take precedence over this mission: to proclaim Christ to all the nations, to speak of his marvelous goodness, to tell of His power to save, and to assure every man and woman that whoever believes in Christ will not die but will have eternal life (cf. Jn. 3:16).

My brothers and sons in Christ, the words of Peter at Caesarea Philippi also have special meaning for you. Your life, too, must be rooted in Christ and built up in Him (cf. Col. 2:7). For it is because of Christ, on account of Christ, and for Christ that you wish to serve the People of God as priests. Thus your knowledge of Christ and your love for Him must continually grow and deepen. You shall have to be men of strong faith who through the Eucharist, the liturgy of the hours and daily personal prayer maintain a vibrant friendship with Jesus, with Jesus who told His disciples: "I no longer speak of you as slaves.... Instead I call you friends" (Jn. 15:15). And so at all times and in all places, your first thoughts must go to Him who is the Christ, the Messiah, the Son of the living God.

2. The feast of the Chair of St. Peter by a happy coincidence is also the birthday of George Washington, your first President. In a certain sense these two events indicate the motivation for my coming here today. It has been my desire as Bishop of Rome to visit the various Colleges of the city, but I have come to the North American College in particular as an extension of my recent

visit to the United States. This evening you represent for me the Church in the United States: you, my brother bishops, and you who make up the community in Rome known as the North American College, on the Janiculum Hill and at Via dell'Umiltá. In all of you and through you I once again greet the people of America.

On this occasion I would like to speak about what I consider to be extremely important components of priestly preparation, and to reiterate several points in this regard which I stressed during my visit to your country.

3. The first priority in seminary life is the Word of God. God's Word is the center of all theological study; it is the chief instrument for handing down Christian doctrine, and it is the perpetual source of spiritual life (cf. Apostolic Constitution *Missale romanum*, April 3, 1969). Speaking to seminarians in America, I said: "The intellectual formation of the priest, which is so vital for the times in which we live, embraces a number of the human sciences as well as the various sacred sciences. These all have an important place in your preparation for the priesthood. But the first priority for seminaries today is the teaching of God's Word in all its purity and integrity, with all its demands and in all its power" (Address at St. Charles Seminary, Philadelphia).

It is my hope that in your reverence for the Word of God you will be like Mary—like Mary whose response to God's word was "Fiat": "Let it be done to me as you say" (Lk. 1:38); like Mary "who trusted that the Lord's words to her would be fulfilled" (Lk. 1:45); like Mary who treasured those things which were said of her Son and pondered them in her heart (cf. Lk. 2:19). May you treasure God's Word always and ponder it each day in your heart, so that your whole life may become a proclamation of Christ, the Word made flesh (cf. Jn. 1:14).

4. The proclamation of God's Word reaches its summit in the celebration of the Eucharist. Indeed, all your personal endeavors and all the activities of the seminary community are bound up with the Eucharistic Sacrifice and directed toward it: "For the most blessed Eucharist contains the Church's entire spiritual wealth, that is, Christ Himself, our Passover and living Bread" *(Presbyterorum ordinis,* no. 5). I strongly urge you, therefore, to make the Mass the real center of your life each day, and I recommend that you regularly spend time in prayer before the Blessed Sacrament, adoring our Lord and Savior Jesus Christ.

5. Seminary life should also be characterized by an atmosphere of recollection, which enables each of you to acquire lifelong habits of study and prayer, and to develop interiorly the attitudes of self-sacrifice, generosity and joyful obedience—attitudes which are so necessary in a priest. For a priest is truly called to put on the mind and heart of Christ (cf. Phil. 2:5), to imitate the Son who "learned obedience from what he suffered" (Heb. 5:8), and to say with Jesus: "I am not seeking my own will but the will of him who sent me" (Jn. 5:30). Sound discipline in the seminary, when it is properly exercised, creates that atmosphere of recollection which helps you prepare for a life of continual conversion and

generous service. In particular it will assist you, as I said in Philadelphia, "in ratifying day after day in your hearts the obedience you owe to Christ and His Church."

6. Ten years ago today, my beloved Predecessor Paul VI visited the North American College. On that occasion he spoke of the special value of preparing for the priesthood here in Rome. "Your being here in Rome," he said, "is neither accidental nor unimportant. It is not pure coincidence.... It is something deliberately willed for your spiritual formation; for your preparation for a priestly ministry; for a service, yet to come, to the Church and to your fellow citizens."

If you sometimes wonder why the American bishops have built and maintained this college in Rome, or why the Catholic faithful of the United States for over a century have given financial support and have sacrificed of themselves to provide for you and many others the opportunity to prepare for the priesthood in Rome, the answer is found in the words of Peter at Caesarea Philippi; it is linked to the mystery of Peter's mission in the universal Church. Here in Rome the universality and rich diversity of the Church are seen more clearly than elsewhere; here the apostolic tradition of the Church as a living reality and not merely as a relic of the past becomes a conscious part of your vision of faith, and here in Rome you encounter the Successor of Peter as he endeavors to show fidelity to Christ by confirming all his brethren in the Faith.

7. I would like to take this occasion to extend a special greeting to Cardinal Baum, who

has only recently come to Rome to assume the weighty task of directing the Sacred Congregation for Catholic Education. Among his many responsibilities will be the promotion of the authentic renewal of seminary life in Rome and throughout the world. No other responsibility of his will be of greater importance. In full accord with this conviction of mine are the following words that I wrote to the bishops of the Church in my Holy Thursday Letter last year: "The full reconstitution of the life of the seminaries throughout the Church will be the best proof of the achievement of the renewal to which the Council directed the Church."

8. Beloved brothers and sons in Christ, you have a special place in my thoughts and prayers, and I look to you with confidence. For I see your youth and your sincerity, your strength and your desire to serve. I see your joy and your love for Christ and His people. All this gives me hope that the authentic renewal of the Church begun by the Second Vatican Council will indeed be brought to completion. Yes, your lives hold great promise for the future of the Church, for the future of the evangelization of the world, provided that you remain faithful: faithful to the Word of God, faithful to the Eucharist, faithful to prayer and study, faithful to the Lord, who has begun this good work in you, and who will carry it through to completion (cf. Phil. 1:6).

Dear brothers and sons: Let us together praise His name, and let us proclaim by word and deed—today and always—that Jesus is the Christ, the Son of the living God.

On the Mystery and Worship of the Eucharist

Dominicae Cenae

Letter to all bishops of the Church on February 24, 1980.

My venerable and dear brothers,

1. Again this year, for Holy Thursday, I am writing a letter to all of you. This letter has an immediate connection with the one which you received last year on the same occasion, together with the letter to the priests. I wish *in the first place to thank you cordially* for having accepted my previous letters with that spirit of unity which the Lord established between us, and also for having transmitted to your priests the thoughts that I desired to express at the beginning of my pontificate.

During the Eucharistic Liturgy of Holy Thursday, you renewed, together with your priests, the promises and commitments undertaken at the moment of ordination. Many of you, venerable and dear brothers, told me about it later, also adding words of personal thanks, and indeed often sending those expressed by your priests.

Furthermore, many priests expressed their joy, both because of the profound and solemn character of Holy Thursday as the annual "feast of priests" and also because of the importance of the subjects dealt with in the letter addressed to them.

Those replies form a rich collection which once more indicates how dear to the vast majority of priests of the Catholic Church is the path of the priestly life, the path along which this Church has been journeying for centuries: how much they love and esteem it, and how much they desire to follow it for the future.

At this point I must add that *only a certain number of matters were dealt with in the letter to priests*, as was in fact emphasized at the beginning of the document.[1] Furthermore, the main stress was laid upon the pastoral character of the priestly ministry; but this certainly does not mean that those groups of priests who are not engaged in direct pastoral activity were not also taken into consideration. In this regard I would refer once more to the teaching of the Second Vatican Council, and also to the declarations of the 1971 Synod of Bishops.

The pastoral character of the priestly ministry does not cease to mark the life of every priest, even if the daily tasks that he carries out are not explicitly directed to the pastoral administration of the sacraments. In this sense, the letter written to the priests on Holy Thursday was addressed to them all, without any exception, even though, as I said above, it did not deal with all the aspects

NATIONAL CONFERENCE OF CATHOLIC BISHOPS
1312 MASSACHUSETTS AVENUE, N.W.
WASHINGTON, D.C. 20005

OFFICE OF THE PRESIDENT

February 15, 1982

To the Rectors, Faculty and Students of the
American Seminaries:

    At the suggestion of His Eminence William Cardinal Baum of the Sacred Congregation for Catholic Education and with my blessing, the Daughters of Saint Paul, working with the Bishops' Committee on Priestly Formation of the United States Catholic Conference, present to the American seminaries and in particular to our American seminarians this edition of the talks of Pope Paul VI and His Holiness Pope John Paul II to seminaries and seminarians.

    From the beginning of his Pontificate, our present Holy Father has indicated over and over again his special predilection for seminarians and in particular his concern for their proper preparation for the work they will undertake as his co-laborers with Christ in the work of bringing God to the world and the world to God.

    I commend to your reading these talks and allocutions, knowing that you will find herein encouragement for your present work and formation and inspiration for the days ahead.

                    Sincerely yours in Christ,

                      + John R. Roach

                    Most Rev. John R. Roach
                    Archbishop of Saint Paul and Minneapolis
                    President, NCCB/USCC

of the life and activity of priests. I think this clarification is useful and opportune at the beginning of the present letter:

I. THE EUCHARISTIC MYSTERY IN THE LIFE OF THE CHURCH AND OF THE PRIEST

Eucharist and Priesthood

2. The present letter that I am addressing to you, my venerable and dear brothers in the episcopate—and which is, as I have said, in a certain way a continuation of the previous one—is also closely linked with the mystery of Holy Thursday, and is related to the priesthood. In fact I intend to devote it to the Eucharist, and in particular *to certain aspects of the Eucharistic Mystery and its impact on the lives of those who are the ministers of it:* and so those to whom this letter is directly addressed are you, the bishops of the Church; together with you, all the priests; and, in their own rank, the deacons too.

In reality, the ministerial and hierarchical priesthood, the priesthood of the bishops and the priests, and, at their side, the ministry of the deacons—ministries which normally begin with the proclamation of the Gospel—are in the closest relationship with the Eucharist. The Eucharist is the principal and central *raison d'être* of the sacrament of the priesthood, which effectively came into being at the moment of the institution of the Eucharist, and together with it.[2] Not without reason the words "Do this in memory of me" are said immediately after the words of Eucharistic Consecration, and we repeat them every time we celebrate the Holy Sacrifice.[3]

Through our ordination—the celebration of which is linked to the holy Mass from the very first liturgical evidence[4]—we are united in a singular and exceptional way to the Eucharist. In a certain way we derive *from* it and exist *for* it. We are also, and in a special way, responsible for it—each priest in his own community and each bishop by virtue of the care of all the communities entrusted to him, on the basis of the *sollicitudo omnium ecclesiarum* that St. Paul speaks of.[5] Thus we bishops and priests are entrusted with the great "Mystery of Faith," and while it is also given to the whole People of God, to all believers in Christ, yet to us has been entrusted the Eucharist also "for" others, who expect from us a particular witness of veneration and love towards this sacrament, so that they too may be able to be built up and vivified "to offer spiritual sacrifices."[6]

In this way our eucharistic worship, both in the celebration of Mass and in our devotion to the Blessed Sacrament, is like a life-giving current that links our ministerial or hierarchical priesthood to the common priesthood of the faithful, and presents it in its vertical dimension and with its central value. The priest fulfills his principal mission and is manifested in all his fullness when he celebrates the Eucharist,[7] and this manifestation is more complete when he himself allows the depth of that mystery to become visible, so that it alone shines forth in people's hearts and minds, through his ministry. This is the supreme exercise of the "kingly priesthood," "the source and summit of all Christian life."[8]

Worship of the Eucharistic Mystery

3. This worship is directed towards God the Father through Jesus Christ in the Holy Spirit. In the first place towards the Father, who, as St. John's Gospel says, "loved the world so much that he gave his only Son, so that everyone who believes in him may not be lost but may have eternal life."[9]

It is also directed, in the Holy Spirit, to the incarnate Son, in the economy of salvation, especially at that moment of supreme dedication and total abandonment of Himself to which the words uttered in the Upper Room refer: "This is my body given up for you.... This is the cup of my blood shed for you...."[10] The liturgical acclamation: "We proclaim your death, Lord Jesus" takes us back precisely to that moment; and with the proclamation of His resurrection we embrace in the same act of veneration Christ risen and glorified "at the right hand of the Father," as also the expectation of His "coming in glory." *Yet it is the voluntary emptying of Himself, accepted by the Father and glorified with the resurrection*, which, sacramentally celebrated together with the resurrection, brings us to adore the Redeemer who "became obedient unto death, even death on a cross."[11]

And this adoration of ours contains yet another special characteristic. It is compenetrated by the greatness of that human death, in which the world, that is to say, each one of us, has been loved "to the end."[12] Thus it is also a response that tries to repay that love immolated even to the death on the cross: it is our "Eucharist," that is to say, our giving Him thanks, our praise of Him for having redeemed us by His death and made us sharers in immortal life through His resurrection.

This worship, given therefore to the Trinity of the Father and of the Son and of the Holy Spirit, above all accompanies and permeates the celebration of the Eucharistic Liturgy. But it must fill our churches also outside the timetable of Masses. Indeed, since the Eucharistic Mystery was instituted out of love, and makes Christ sacramentally present, it is worthy of thanksgiving and worship. And this worship must be prominent in all our encounters with the Blessed Sacrament, both when we visit our churches and when the sacred Species are taken to the sick and administered to them.

Adoration of Christ in this sacrament of love must also find expression *in various forms of Eucharistic devotion:* personal prayer before the Blessed Sacrament, Hours of Adoration, periods of exposition—short, prolonged and annual (Forty Hours)—Eucharistic benediction, Eucharistic processions, Eucharistic congresses.[13] A particular mention should be made at this point of the Solemnity of the Body and Blood of Christ as an act of public worship rendered to Christ present in the Eucharist, a feast instituted by my Predecessor Urban IV in memory of the institution of this great Mystery.[14] All this therefore corresponds to the general principles and particular norms already long in existence but newly formulated during or after the Second Vatican Council.[15]

The encouragement and the deepening of Eucharistic worship are *proofs of that authentic renewal* which the Council set itself as an aim and of which they are *the central point.* And this, venerable and dear brothers, deserves separate reflection. The Church and the world have a great need of Eucharistic worship. Jesus waits for us in this sacrament of love. Let us be generous with our time in going to meet Him in adoration and in contemplation that is full of faith and ready to make reparation for the great faults and crimes of the world. May our adoration never cease.

Eucharist and Church

4. Thanks to the Council we have realized with renewed force the following truth: Just as the Church "makes the Eucharist" so "the Eucharist builds up" the Church[16]; and this truth is closely bound up with the mystery of Holy Thursday. The Church was founded, as the new community of the People of God, in the apostolic community of those Twelve who, at the Last Supper, became partakers of the body and blood of the Lord under the species of bread and wine. Christ had said to them: "Take and eat.... Take and drink." And carrying out this command of His, they entered for the first time into sacramental communion with the Son of God, a communion that is a pledge of eternal life. From that

moment until the end of time, *the Church is being built up through that same communion with the Son of God, a communion which is a pledge of the eternal Passover.*

Dear and venerable brothers in the episcopate, as teachers and custodians of the salvific truth of the Eucharist, we must always and everywhere preserve this meaning and this dimension of the sacramental encounter and intimacy with Christ. It is precisely these elements which constitute the very substance of Eucharistic worship. The meaning of the truth expounded above in no way diminishes—in fact, it facilitates—the Eucharistic character of spiritual drawing together and union between the people who share in the sacrifice, which then in Communion becomes for them the banquet. This drawing together and this union, the prototype of which is the union of the Apostles about Christ at the Last Supper, express the Church and bring her into being.

But the Church is not brought into being only through the union of people, through the experience of brotherhood to which the Eucharistic Banquet gives rise. The Church is brought into being when, in that fraternal union and communion, we celebrate the sacrifice of the cross of Christ, when we proclaim "the Lord's death until he comes,"[17] and later, when, being deeply compenetrated with the mystery of our salvation, we approach as a community the table of the Lord, in order to be nourished there, in a sacramental manner, by the fruits of the Holy Sacrifice of propitiation. Therefore in Eucharistic Communion we receive Christ, Christ Himself; and our union with Him, which is a gift and grace for each individual, brings it about that in Him we are also associated in the unity of His Body which is the Church.

Only in this way, through that faith and that disposition of mind, is there brought about that building up of the Church, which in the Eucharist truly finds its "source and summit," according to the well-known expression of the Second Vatican Council.[18] This truth, which as a result of the same Council has received a new and vigorous emphasis,[19] must be a frequent theme of our reflection and teaching. Let all pastoral activity be nourished by it, and may it also be food for ourselves and for all the priests who collaborate with us, and likewise for the whole of the communities entrusted to us. In this practice there should thus be revealed, almost at every step, that *close relationship between the Church's spiritual and apostolic vitality* and *the Eucharist, understood in its profound significance* and from all points of view.[20]

Eucharist and Charity

5. Before proceeding to more detailed observations on the subject of the celebration of the Holy Sacrifice, I wish briefly to reaffirm the fact that Eucharistic worship constitutes the soul of all Christian life. In fact, Christian life is expressed in the fulfilling of the greatest commandment, that is to say, in the love of God and

neighbor, and this love finds its source in the Blessed Sacrament, which is commonly called the sacrament of love.

The Eucharist signifies this charity, and therefore recalls it, makes it present *and at the same time brings it about.* Every time that we consciously share in it, there opens in our souls a real dimension of that unfathomable love that includes everything that God has done and continues to do for us human beings, as Christ says: "My Father goes on working, and so do I."[21] Together with this unfathomable and free gift, which is *charity* revealed in its fullest degree in the saving sacrifice of the Son of God, the sacrifice of which the Eucharist is the indelible sign, there also springs up within us a lively response of love. We not only know love; we ourselves *begin to love.* We enter, so to speak, upon the path of love and along this path make progress. Thanks to the Eucharist, the love that springs up within us from the Eucharist develops in us, becomes deeper and grows stronger.

Eucharistic worship is, therefore, precisely the expression of that love which is the authentic and deepest characteristic of the Christian vocation. This worship springs from the love and serves the love to which we are all called in Jesus Christ.[22] A living fruit of this worship is the perfecting of the image of God that we bear within us, an image that corresponds to the one that Christ has revealed in us. As we thus become adorers of the Father "in spirit and truth,"[23] we mature in an ever fuller union with Christ, we are ever more united to Him, and—if one may use the expression—we are ever more in harmony with Him.

The doctrine of the Eucharist, sign of unity and bond of charity, taught by St. Paul,[24] has been in subsequent times deepened by the writings of very many saints who are living examples for us of Eucharistic worship. We must always have this reality before our eyes, and at the same time we must continually try to bring it about that our own generation too may add new examples to those marvelous examples of the past, new examples no less living and eloquent, that will reflect the age to which we belong.

Eucharist and Neighbor

6. *The authentic sense of the Eucharist becomes of itself the school of active love for neighbor.* We know that this is the true and full order of love that the Lord has taught us: "By this love you have for one another, everyone will know that you are my disciples."[25] The Eucharist educates us to this love in a deeper way; it shows us, in fact, what value each person, our brother or sister, has in God's eyes, if Christ offers Himself equally to each one, under the species of bread and wine. If our Eucharistic worship is authentic, it must make us grow in awareness of the dignity of each person. The awareness of that dignity becomes the *deepest motive of our relationship with our neighbor.*

We must also become particularly sensitive to all human suffering and misery, to all injustice and wrong, and seek the way to redress them effectively. Let us learn to discover with respect the truth about the inner self that becomes the dwelling place of God present in the Eucharist. Christ comes into the hearts of our brothers and sisters and visits their consciences. How the image of each and every one changes, when we become aware of this reality, when we make it the subject of our reflections! The sense of the Eucharistic Mystery leads us to a love for our neighbor, to a love for every human being.[26]

Eucharist and Life

7. Since, therefore, the Eucharist is the source of charity, it has always been at the center of the life of Christ's disciples. It has the appearance of bread and wine, that is to say, of food and drink; it is, therefore, as familiar to people, as closely linked to their life, as food and drink. The veneration of God, who is love, springs, in Eucharistic worship, from that kind of intimacy in which *He Himself, by analogy with food and drink, fills our spiritual being,* ensuring its life, as food and drink do. This "Eucharistic" veneration of God therefore strictly corresponds to His saving plan. He Himself, the Father, wants the "true worshipers"[27] to worship Him precisely in this way, and it is Christ who expresses this desire, both with His words and likewise with this sacrament in which He makes possible worship of the Father in the way most in conformity with the Father's will.

From this concept of Eucharistic worship there then stems the whole *sacramental style of the Christian's life.* In fact, leading a life based on the sacraments and animated by the common priesthood means in the first place that Christians desire God to act in them in order to enable them to attain, in the Spirit, "the fullness of Christ himself."[28] God, on His part, does not touch them only through events and by this inner grace; He also acts in them with greater certainty and power through the sacraments. The sacraments give the lives of Christians a sacramental style.

Now, of all the sacraments it is the Holy Eucharist that brings to fullness their initiation as Christians and confers upon the exercise of the common priesthood that sacramental and ecclesial form that links it—as we mentioned before[29]—to the exercise of the ministerial priesthood. In this way Eucharistic worship is the *center and goal of all sacramental life.*[30] In the depths of Eucharistic worship we find a continual echo of the sacraments of Christian initiation: Baptism and Confirmation. Where better is there expressed the truth that we are not only "called God's children" but "that is what we are"[31] by virtue of the sacrament of Baptism, if not precisely in the fact that in the Eucharist we become partakers of the body and blood of God's only Son? And what predisposes us more to be "true witnesses of Christ"[32] before the world—as we are enabled to be by the sacrament of Confirmation—than Eucharistic Communion, in which Christ bears witness to us, and we to Him?

It is impossible to analyze here in greater detail the links between the Eucharist and the other sacraments, in particular with the sacrament of family life and the sacrament of the sick. In the encyclical *Redemptor hominis*[33] I have already drawn attention to the close link between the sacrament of Penance and the sacrament of the Eucharist. *It is not only that Penance leads to the Eucharist, but that the Eucharist also leads to Penance.* For when we realize who it is that we receive in Eucharistic Communion, there springs up in us almost spontaneously a sense of unworthiness, together with sorrow for our sins and an interior need for purification.

But we must always take care that this great meeting with Christ in the Eucharist does not become a mere habit, and that we do not receive Him unworthily, that is to say, in a state of mortal sin. The practice of the virtue of penance and the sacrament of Penance are essential for sustaining in us and continually deepening that spirit of veneration which man owes to God Himself and to His love so marvelously revealed. The purpose of these words is to put forward some general reflections on worship of the Eucharistic Mystery, and they could be developed at greater length and more fully. In particular, it would be possible to link what has been said about the effects of the Eucharist on love for others with what we have just noted about commitments undertaken towards humanity and the Church in Eucharistic Communion, and then outline the picture of that "new earth"[34] that springs from the Eucharist through every "new self."[35] *In this sacrament* of bread and wine, of food and drink, *everything that is human really undergoes a singular transformation and elevation.* Eucharistic worship is not so much worship of the inaccessible transcendence as worship of the divine condescension, and it is also the merciful and redeeming transformation of the world in the human heart.

Recalling all this only very briefly, I wish, notwithstanding this brevity, to create a wider context for the questions that I shall subsequently have to deal with: These questions are closely linked with the celebration of the Holy Sacrifice. In fact, in that celebration there is expressed in a more direct way the worship of the Eucharist. This worship comes from the heart, as a most precious homage inspired by the faith, hope and charity which were infused into us at Baptism. And it is precisely about this that I wish to write to you in this letter, venerable and dear brothers in the episcopate, and with you to the priests and deacons. It will be followed by detailed indications from the Sacred Congregation for the Sacraments and Divine Worship.

II. THE SACRED CHARACTER OF THE EUCHARIST AND SACRIFICE

Sacred Character

8. Beginning with the Upper Room and Holy Thursday, the celebration of the Eucharist has a long history, a history as long as that of the Church. In the course of this history the secondary elements have undergone certain changes,

but there has been no change in the essence of the "Mysterium" instituted by the Redeemer of the world at the Last Supper. The Second Vatican Council too brought alterations, as a result of which the present liturgy of the Mass is different in some ways from the one known before the Council. We do not intend to speak of these differences: It is better that we should now concentrate on what is essential and immutable in the Eucharistic Liturgy.

There is a close link between this element of the Eucharist and its sacredness, that is to say, its being a holy and sacred action. Holy and sacred, because in it are the continual presence and action of Christ, "the Holy One" of God,[36] "anointed with the Holy Spirit,"[37] "consecrated by the Father"[38] to lay down His life of His own accord and to take it up again,[39] and the High Priest of the New Covenant.[40] For it is He who, represented by the celebrant, makes His entrance into the sanctuary and proclaims His Gospel. It is He who is "the offerer and the offered, the consecrator and the consecrated."[41] The Eucharist is a holy and sacred action, because it constitutes the sacred Species, the *Sancta sanctis*, that is to say, the "holy things (Christ, the Holy One) given to the holy," as all the Eastern liturgies sing at the moment when the Eucharistic Bread is raised in order to invite the faithful to the Lord's Supper.

The sacredness of the Mass, therefore, is not a "sacralization," that is to say, something that man adds to Christ's action in the Upper Room, for the Holy Thursday supper was a sacred rite, a primary and constitutive liturgy, through which Christ, by pledging to give His life for us, Himself celebrated sacramentally the mystery of His passion and resurrection, the heart of every Mass. Our Masses, being derived from this liturgy, possess of themselves a complete liturgical form, which, in spite of its variations in line with the families of rites, remains substantially the same. The sacred character of the Mass is a sacredness instituted by Christ. The words and actions of every priest, answered by the conscious active participation of the whole Eucharistic assembly, echo the words and actions of Holy Thursday.

The priest offers the Holy Sacrifice *in persona Christi;* this means more than offering "in the name of" or "in place of" Christ. *In persona* means in specific sacramental identification with "the eternal High Priest"[42] who is the author and principal subject of this sacrifice of His, a sacrifice in which, in truth, nobody can take His place. Only He—only Christ—was able and is always able to be the true and effective "expiation for our sins and...for the sins of the whole world."[43] Only His sacrifice—and no one else's —was able and is able to have a "propitiatory power" before God, the Trinity, and the transcendent holiness. Awareness of this reality throws a certain light on the character and significance of the priest celebrant who, *by confecting the Holy Sacrifice and acting "in persona Christi,"* is sacramentally (and ineffably) brought into that most profound *sacredness,* and made part of it, spiritually linking with it in turn all those participating in the Eucharistic assembly.

This sacred rite, which is actuated in different liturgical forms, may lack some secondary elements, but it can in no way lack its essential sacred character and sacramentality, since these are willed by Christ and transmitted and regulated by the Church. Neither can this sacred rite be utilized for other ends. If separated from its distinctive sacrificial and sacramental nature, the Eucharistic Mystery simply ceases to be. It admits of no "profane" imitation, an imitation that would very easily (indeed regularly) become a profanation. This must always be remembered, perhaps above all in our time, when we see a tendency to do away with the distinction between the "sacred" and "profane," given the widespread tendency, at least in some places, to desacralize everything.

In view of this fact, *the Church has a special duty to safeguard and strengthen the sacredness of the Eucharist.* In our pluralistic and often deliberately secularized society, *the living faith* of the Christian community—a faith always aware of its rights vis-à-vis those who do not share that faith—ensures respect for this sacredness. The duty to respect each person's faith is the complement of the natural and civil right to freedom of conscience and of religion.

The sacred character of the Eucharist has found and continues to find expression in the terminology of theology and the liturgy.[44] This sense of the objective sacred character of the

Eucharistic Mystery is so much part of the faith of the People of God that their faith is enriched and strengthened by it.[45] Therefore the ministers of the Eucharist must, especially today, be illumined by the fullness of this living faith, and in its light they must understand and perform all that is part, by Christ's will and the will of His Church, of their priestly ministry.

Sacrifice

9. The Eucharist is above all else a sacrifice. It is the sacrifice of the redemption and also the sacrifice of the New Covenant,[46] as we believe and as the Eastern Churches clearly profess: "Today's sacrifice," the Greek Church stated centuries ago, "is like that offered once by the Only-begotten Incarnate Word; it is offered by Him (now as then), since it is one and the same sacrifice."[47] Accordingly, precisely by making this single sacrifice of our salvation present, man and the world are restored to God through the paschal newness of redemption. This restoration cannot cease to be: it is the foundation of the "new and eternal covenant" of God with man and of man with God. If it were missing, one would have to question both the excellence of the sacrifice of the redemption, which in fact was perfect and definitive, and also the sacrificial value of the Mass. In fact, the Eucharist, being a true sacrifice, brings about this restoration to God.

Consequently, the celebrant, as minister of this sacrifice, is the authentic *priest,* performing—in virtue of the specific power of sacred ordination—a true sacrificial act that brings creation back to God. Although all those who participate in the Eucharist do not confect the sacrifice as he does, they offer with him, by virtue of the common priesthood, their own *spiritual sacrifices* represented by the bread and wine from the moment of their presentation at the altar. For this liturgical action, which takes a solemn form in almost all liturgies, has a "spiritual value and meaning."[48] The bread and wine become in a sense a symbol of all that the Eucharistic assembly brings, on its own part as an offering to God, and offers spiritually.

It is important that this first moment of the Liturgy of the Eucharist in the strict sense should find expression in the attitude of the participants. There is a link between this and the offertory "procession" provided for in the recent liturgical reform[49] and accompanied, in keeping with ancient tradition, by a psalm or song. A certain length of time must be allowed, so that all can become aware of this act, which is given expression at the same time by the words of the celebrant.

Awareness of the act of presenting the offerings should be maintained throughout the Mass. Indeed, it should be brought to fullness at the moment of the consecration and of the anamnesis offering, as is demanded by the fundamental value of the moment of the sacrifice. This is shown by the words of the Eucharistic Prayer said aloud by the priest. It seems worthwhile repeating here some expressions in the Third

Eucharistic Prayer that show in particular the sacrificial character of the Eucharist and link the offering of our persons with Christ's offering: "Look with favor on your Church's offering, and see the Victim whose death has reconciled us to yourself. Grant that we, who are nourished by his body and blood, may be filled with his Holy Spirit, and become one body, one spirit in Christ. May he make us an everlasting gift to you."

This sacrificial value is expressed earlier in every celebration by the words with which the priest concludes the presentation of the gifts, asking the faithful to pray "that my sacrifice and yours may be acceptable to God, the almighty Father." These words are binding, since they express the character of the entire Eucharistic Liturgy and the fullness of its divine and ecclesial content.

All who participate with faith in the Eucharist become aware that it is a "sacrifice," that is to say, a "consecrated offering." For the bread and wine presented at the altar and accompanied by the devotion and the spiritual sacrifices of the participants are finally consecrated, so as to become *truly, really and substantially* Christ's own body that is given up and His blood that is shed. Thus, by virtue of the consecration, the species of bread and wine re-present[50] in a sacramental, unbloody manner the bloody propitiatory sacrifice offered by Him on the cross to His Father for the salvation of the world. Indeed, He alone, giving Himself as a propitiatory victim in an act of supreme surrender and immolation, has reconciled humanity with the Father, solely through His sacrifice, "having cancelled the bond which stood against us."[51]

To this sacrifice, which is renewed in a sacramental form on the altar, the offerings of bread and wine, united with the devotion of the faithful, nevertheless bring their unique contribution, since by means of the consecration by the priest they become sacred Species. This is made clear by the way in which the priest acts during the Eucharistic Prayer, especially at the consecration, and when the celebration of the Holy Sacrifice and participation in it are accompanied by awareness that "the Teacher is here and is calling for you."[52] This call of the Lord to us through His sacrifice opens our hearts, so that, purified in the mystery of our redemption, they may be united to Him in Eucharistic Communion, which confers upon participation at Mass a value that is mature, complete and binding on human life: "The Church's intention is that the faithful not only offer the spotless victim but also learn to offer themselves and daily to be drawn into ever more perfect union, through Christ the Mediator, with the Father and with each other, so that at last God may be all in all."[53]

It is therefore very opportune and necessary to continue to actuate a new and intense education, in order to discover all the richness contained in the new liturgy. Indeed, the liturgical renewal that has taken place since the Second Vatican Council has given, so to speak, greater visibility to *the Eucharistic Sacrifice.* One factor contributing to this is that the words of the Eucharistic Prayer are said aloud by the celebrant, particularly the words of consecration, with the acclamation by the assembly immediately after the elevation.

All this should fill us with joy, but we should also remember that *these changes demand new spiritual awareness and maturity,* both on the part of the celebrant—especially now that he celebrates "facing the people"—and by the faithful. Eucharistic worship matures and grows when the words of the Eucharistic Prayer, especially the words of consecration, are spoken with great humility and simplicity, in a worthy and fitting way, which is understandable and in keeping with their holiness; when this essential act of the Eucharistic Liturgy is performed unhurriedly; and when it brings about in us such recollection and devotion that the participants become aware of the greatness of the mystery being accomplished and show it by their attitude.

III. THE TWO TABLES OF THE LORD AND THE COMMON POSSESSION OF THE CHURCH

The Table of the Word of God

10. We are well aware that from the earliest times the celebration of the Eucharist has been linked not only with prayer but also with the

reading of Sacred Scripture and with singing by the whole assembly. As a result, it has long been possible to apply to the Mass the comparison, made by the Fathers, with the two tables, at which the Church prepares for her children the Word of God and the Eucharist, that is, the Bread of the Lord. We must therefore go back to the first part of the Sacred Mystery, the part that at present is most often called the *Liturgy of the Word,* and devote some attention to it.

The reading of the passages of Sacred Scripture chosen for each day *has been subjected by the Council* to new criteria and requirements.[54] As a result of these norms of the Council a new collection of readings has been made, in which there has been applied to some extent the principle of continuity of texts and the principle of making all the sacred books accessible. The insertion of the Psalms with responses into the liturgy makes the participants familiar with the great wealth of Old Testament prayer and poetry. The fact that these texts are read and sung in the vernacular enables everyone to participate with fuller understanding.

Nevertheless, there are also those people who, having been educated on the basis of the old liturgy in Latin, experience the lack of this "one language," which in all the world was an expression of the unity of the Church and through its dignified character elicited a profound sense of the Eucharistic Mystery. It is therefore necessary to show not only understanding but also full respect towards these sentiments and desires. As far as possible these sentiments and desires are to be accommodated, as is moreover provided for in the new dispositions.[55] The Roman Church has special obligations towards Latin, the splendid language of ancient Rome, and she must manifest them whenever the occasion presents itself.

The possibilities that the post-conciliar renewal has introduced in this respect are indeed often utilized so as to make us *witnesses of and sharers in the authentic celebration of the Word of God.* There is also an increase in the number of people taking an active part in this celebration. Groups of readers and cantors, and still more often choirs of men or women, are being set up and are devoting themselves with great enthusiasm to this aspect. The Word of God, Sacred Scripture, is beginning to take on new life in many Christian communities. The faithful gathered for the liturgy prepare with song for listening to the Gospel, which is proclaimed with the devotion and love due to it.

All this is noted with great esteem and gratitude, but it must not be forgotten that complete renewal makes yet other demands. These demands consist in *a new sense of responsibility towards the Word of God* transmitted through the liturgy in various languages, something that is certainly in keeping with the universality of the Gospel and its purposes. The same sense of responsibility also involves the performance of the corresponding liturgical actions (reading or singing), which must accord with the principles of art. To preserve these actions from all artificiality, they should express such capacity, simplicity and dignity as to highlight the special character of the sacred text, even by the very manner of reading or singing.

Accordingly, these demands, which spring from a new responsibility for the Word of God in the liturgy,[56] go yet deeper and *concern the inner attitude* with which the ministers of the Word perform their function in the liturgical assembly.[57] This responsibility also concerns *the choice of texts. The choice has already been made by the competent ecclesiastical authority, which has also made provision for the cases in which readings more suited to a particular situation may be chosen.*[58] Furthermore, it must always be remembered that only the Word of God can be used for Mass readings. The reading of Scripture cannot be replaced by the reading of other texts, however much they may be endowed with undoubted religious and moral values. On the other hand, such texts can be used very profitably in the homily. Indeed the homily is supremely suitable for the use of such texts, provided that their content corresponds to the required conditions, since it is one of the tasks that belong to the nature of the homily to show the points of convergence between revealed divine wisdom and noble human thought seeking the truth by various paths.

The Table of the Bread of the Lord

11. The other table of the Eucharistic Mystery, that of the Bread of the Lord, also requires reflection from the viewpoint of the present-day liturgical renewal. This is a question

of the greatest importance, since it concerns a special act of living faith, and indeed, as has been attested since the earliest centuries,[59] it is a manifestation of *worship of Christ, who in Eucharistic Communion entrusts Himself to each one of us,* to our hearts, our consciences, our lips and our mouths, in the form of food. Therefore there is special need, with regard to this question, for the watchfulness spoken of by the Gospel, on the part of the pastors who have charge of Eucharistic worship and on the part of the People of God, whose "sense of the faith"[60] must be very alert and acute particularly in this area.

I therefore wish to entrust this question to the heart of each one of you, venerable and dear brothers in the episcopate. You must above all make it part of your care for all the Churches entrusted to you. I ask this of you in the name of the unity that we have received from the Apostles as our heritage, collegial unity. This unity came to birth, in a sense, at the table of the Bread of the Lord on Holy Thursday. With the help of your brothers in the priesthood, do all you can to *safeguard the sacred dignity of the Eucharistic ministry and that deep spirit of Eucharistic Communion* which belongs in a special way to the Church as the People of God, and which is also a particular heritage transmitted to us from the Apostles, by various liturgical traditions, and by unnumbered generations of the faithful, who were often heroic witnesses to Christ, educated in "the school of the cross" (redemption) and of the Eucharist.

It must be remembered that the Eucharist as the table of the Bread of the Lord is a continuous invitation. This is *shown in the liturgy when the celebrant says: "This is the Lamb of God. Happy are those who are called to his supper"*[61]; it is also shown by the familiar Gospel parable about the guests invited to the marriage banquet.[62] Let us remember that in this parable there are many who excuse themselves from accepting the invitation for various reasons.

Moreover our Catholic communities certainly do not lack people who *could participate* in Eucharistic Communion *and do not,* even though they have no serious sin on their conscience as an obstacle. To tell the truth, this attitude, which in some people is linked with an exaggerated severity, has changed in the present century, though it is still to be found here and there. In fact, what one finds most often is not so much a feeling of unworthiness as a certain lack of interior willingness, if one may use this expression, a lack of Eucharistic "hunger" and "thirst," which is also a sign of lack of adequate sensitivity towards the great sacrament of love and a lack of understanding of its nature.

However, we also find in recent years another phenomenon. Sometimes, indeed quite frequently, everybody participating in the Eucharistic assembly goes to Communion; and on some such occasions, as experienced pastors confirm, there has not been due care to approach the sacrament of Penance so as to purify one's conscience. This can of course mean that those approaching the Lord's table find nothing on their conscience, according to the objective law of God, to keep them from this sublime and joyful act of being sacramentally united with Christ. But there can also be, at least at times, another idea behind this: the idea of the Mass as *only* a banquet[63] in which one shares by *receiving the body of Christ in order to manifest, above all else, fraternal communion*. It is not hard to add to these reasons a certain human respect and mere "conformity."

This phenomenon demands from us watchful attention and a theological and pastoral analysis guided by a sense of great responsibility. We cannot allow the life of our communities to lose the good quality of sensitiveness of Christian conscience, guided solely by respect for Christ, who, when He is received in the Eucharist, should find in the heart of each of us a worthy abode. This question is closely linked not only with the practice of the sacrament of Penance but also with a correct sense of responsibility for the whole deposit of moral teaching and for the precise distinction between good and evil, a distinction which then becomes for each person sharing in the Eucharist the basis for a correct judgment of self to be made in the depths of the personal conscience. St. Paul's words, "Let a man examine himself,"[64] are well known; this judgment is an indispensable condition for a personal decision whether to approach Eucharistic Communion or to abstain.

Celebration of the Eucharist places before us many other requirements regarding the ministry of the Eucharistic table. Some of these requirements concern only priests and deacons, others concern all who participate in the Eucharistic Liturgy. Priests and deacons must remember that the service of the table of the Bread of the Lord imposes on them special obligations which refer in the first place to Christ Himself *present in the Eucharist* and secondly to all who actually participate in the Eucharist or who might do so. With regard to the first, perhaps it will not be superfluous to recall the words of the *Pontificale* which on the day of ordination the bishop addresses to the new priest as he hands to him on the paten and in the chalice the bread and wine offered by the faithful and prepared by the deacon: *"Accipe oblationem plebis sanctae Deo offerendam. Agnosce quod agis, imitare quod tractabis, et vitam tuam mysterio dominicae crucis conforma."*[65] This last admonition made to him by the bishop should remain as one of the most precious norms of his Eucharistic ministry.

It is from this admonition that the priest's attitude in handling the bread and wine which have become the body and blood of the Redeemer should draw its inspiration. Thus it is necessary for all of us who are ministers of the Eucharist to examine carefully our actions at the altar, in particular the way in which we handle that food and drink which are the body and blood of the Lord our God in our hands: the way in which we distribute Holy Communion; the way in which we perform the purification.

All these actions have a meaning of their own. Naturally, scrupulosity must be avoided, but God preserve us from behaving in a way that lacks respect, from undue hurry, from an impatience that causes scandal. Over and above our commitment to the evangelical mission, our greatest commitment consists in exercising this mysterious power over the body of the Redeemer, and all that is within us should be decisively ordered to this. We should also always remember that to this ministerial power we have been sacramentally consecrated, that we have been chosen from among men "for the good of men."[66] We especially, the priests of the Latin Church, whose ordination rite added in the course of the centuries the custom of anointing the priest's hands, should think about this.

In some countries *the practice of receiving Communion in the hand* has been introduced. This practice has been requested by individual episcopal conferences and has received approval from the Apostolic See. However, cases of a deplorable lack of respect towards the Eucharistic Species have been reported, cases which are imputable not only to the individuals guilty of such behavior but also to the pastors of the Church who have not been vigilant enough regarding the attitude of the faithful towards the Eucharist. It also happens, on occasion, that the free choice of those who prefer to continue the practice of receiving the Eucharist on the tongue is not taken into account in those places where the distribution of Communion in the hand has been authorized. It is therefore difficult in the context of this present letter not to mention the sad phenomena previously referred to. This is in no way meant to refer to those who, receiving the Lord Jesus in the hand, do so with profound reverence and devotion, in those countries where this practice has been authorized.

But one must not forget the primary office of priests, who have been consecrated by their ordination to represent Christ the Priest: for this reason their hands, like their words and their will, have become the direct instruments of Christ. Through this fact, that is, as ministers of the Holy Eucharist, they have a primary responsibility for the sacred Species, because it is a total responsibility: They offer the bread and wine; they consecrate it, and then distribute the sacred Species to the participants in the assembly who wish to receive them. Deacons can only bring to the altar the offerings of the faithful and, once they have been consecrated by the priest, distribute them. How eloquent, therefore, even if not of ancient custom, is the rite of the anointing of the hands in our Latin ordination, as though precisely for these hands a special grace and power of the Holy Spirit is necessary!

To touch the sacred Species and *to distribute them with their own hands* is a privilege of the ordained, one which indicates an active participation *in the ministry of the Eucharist.* It is obvious that the Church can grant this faculty to those who are neither priests nor deacons, as is the case with acolytes in the exercise of their ministry, especially if they are destined for future ordination, or with other lay people who are chosen for this to meet a just need, but always after an adequate preparation.

A Common Possession of the Church

12. We cannot, even for a moment, forget that the Eucharist is a special possession belonging to the whole Church. It is the *greatest gift* in the order of grace and of sacrament that the divine Spouse has offered and unceasingly offers to His spouse. And precisely because it is such a gift, all of us should in a spirit of profound faith let ourselves be guided by a sense of truly Christian responsibility. A gift obliges us ever more profoundly because it speaks to us not so much with the force of a strict right as with the force of personal confidence, and thus—without legal obligations—it calls for *trust and gratitude.* The Eucharist is just such a gift and such a possession. We should remain faithful in every detail to what it expresses in itself and to what it asks of us, namely, thanksgiving.

The Eucharist is a common possession of the whole Church as the sacrament of her unity. And thus the Church has the strict duty to specify everything which concerns participation in it and its celebration. We should, therefore, act according to the principles laid down by the last Council, which, in the Constitution on the Sacred Liturgy, defined the authorizations and obligations of individual bishops in their dioceses and of the episcopal conferences, given the fact that both act in collegial unity with the Apostolic See.

Furthermore we should follow the directives issued by the various departments of the Holy See in this field: be it in liturgical matters, in the rules established by the liturgical books in what concerns the Eucharistic Mystery,[67] and in the Instructions devoted to this Mystery; be it with regard to *communicatio in sacris,* in the norms of the *Directorium de re oecumenica*[68] and in the *Instructio de peculiaribus casibus admittendi alios christianos ad communionem eucharisticam in Ecclesia catholica.*[69] And although at this stage of renewal the possibility of a certain "creative" freedom has been permitted, nevertheless this freedom must strictly respect the requirements of substantial unity. We can follow the path of this pluralism (which arises in part from the introduction itself of the various languages into the liturgy) only as long as the essential characteristics of the celebration of the Eucharist are preserved, and the norms prescribed by the recent liturgical reform are respected.

Indispensable effort is required everywhere to ensure that within the pluralism of Eucharistic worship envisioned by the Second Vatican Council the unity of which the Eucharist is the sign and cause is clearly manifested.

This task, over which in the nature of things the Apostolic See must keep careful watch, should be assumed not only by each *episcopal conference* but by every minister of the Eucharist, without exception. Each one should also remember that he is responsible for the common good of the whole Church. The *priest as minister,* as celebrant, as the one who presides over the Eucharistic assembly of the faithful, should have a special *sense of the common good of the Church,* which he represents through his ministry, but to which he must also be subordinate, according to a correct discipline of faith. He cannot consider himself a "proprietor" who can make free use of the liturgical text and of the sacred rite as if it were his own property, in such a way as to stamp it with his own arbitrary personal style. At times this latter might seem more effective, and it may better correspond to subjective piety; nevertheless, objectively it is always a betrayal of that union which should find its proper expression in the sacrament of unity.

Every priest who offers the Holy Sacrifice should recall that during this Sacrifice it is not *only* he with his community that is praying but the whole Church, which is thus expressing in this sacrament her spiritual unity, among other ways by the use of the approved liturgical text. To call this position "mere insistence on uniformity" would only show ignorance of the objective requirements of authentic unity, and would be a symptom of harmful individualism.

This subordination of the minister, of the celebrant, to the *Mysterium* which has been entrusted to him by the Church for the good of the whole People of God, should also find expression in the observance of the liturgical requirements concerning the celebration of the Holy Sacrifice. These refer, for example, to dress, and in particular to the vestments worn by the celebrant. Circumstances have of course existed and continue to exist in which the prescriptions do not oblige. We have been greatly moved when reading books written by priests who had been prisoners in extermination camps, with descriptions of Eucharistic Celebrations without the above-mentioned rules, that is to say, without an altar and without vestments. But although in those conditions this was a proof of heroism and deserved profound admiration, nevertheless, in *normal conditions* to ignore the liturgical directives can be interpreted as a lack of respect towards the Eucharist, dictated perhaps by individualism or by an absence of a critical sense concerning current opinions, or by a certain *lack of a spirit of faith*.

Upon all of us who, through the *grace* of God, are ministers of the Eucharist, there weighs a particular responsibility for the ideas and attitudes of our brothers and sisters who have been entrusted to our pastoral care. It is our vocation to nurture, above all by personal example, every healthy manifestation of worship towards Christ present and operative in that sacrament of love. May God preserve us from acting otherwise and weakening that worship by "becoming unaccustomed" to various manifestations and forms of Eucharistic worship which express a perhaps "traditional" but healthy piety, and which express above all that "sense of the faith" possessed by the whole People of God, as the Second Vatican Council recalled.[70]

As I bring these considerations to an end, I would like to ask forgiveness—in my own name and in the name of all of you, venerable and dear brothers in the episcopate—for everything which, for whatever reason, through whatever human weakness, impatience or negligence, and also through the at times partial, one-sided and erroneous application of the directives of the Second Vatican Council, may have caused scandal and disturbance concerning the interpretation of the doctrine and the veneration due to this great sacrament. And I pray the Lord Jesus that in the future we may avoid in our manner of dealing with this Sacred Mystery anything which could weaken or disorient in any way the sense of reverence and love that exists in our faithful people.

May Christ Himself help us to follow the path of true renewal towards that fullness of life and of Eucharistic worship whereby the Church is built up in that unity that she already possesses, and which she desires to bring to ever greater perfection for the glory of the living God and for the salvation of all humanity.

Conclusion

13. Permit me, venerable and dear brothers, to end these reflections of mine, which have been restricted to a detailed examination of only a few questions. In undertaking these reflections, I have had before my eyes all the work carried out by the Second Vatican Council, and have kept in mind Paul VI's encyclical *Mysterium Fidei*, promulgated during that Council, and all the documents issued after the same Council for the purpose of implementing the post-conciliar liturgical renewal. A very close and organic *bond exists between the renewal of the liturgy and the renewal of the whole life of the Church.*

The Church not only acts but also expresses herself in the liturgy, lives by the liturgy and draws from the liturgy the strength for her life. For this reason liturgical renewal carried out correctly in the spirit of the Second Vatican Council is, in a certain sense, the measure and the condition for putting into effect the teaching of that Council which we wish to accept with profound faith, convinced as we are that by means of this Council the Holy Spirit "has spoken to the Church" the truths and given the indications for carrying out her mission among the people of today and tomorrow.

We shall continue in the future to take special care to promote and follow the renewal of the Church according to the teaching of the Second Vatican Council, *in the spirit of an ever-living Tradition.* In fact, to the substance of Tradition properly understood belongs also a correct re-reading of the "signs of the times," which require us to draw from the rich treasure of Revelation "things both new and old."[71] Acting in this spirit, in accordance with this counsel of the Gospel, the Second Vatican Council carried out a providential effort to renew the face of the Church in the sacred liturgy, most often having recourse to what is "ancient," what comes from the heritage of the Fathers and is the expression of the faith and doctrine of a Church which has remained united for so many centuries.

In order to be able to continue in the future to put into practice the directives of the Council in the field of liturgy, and in particular in the field of Eucharistic worship, *close collaboration is necessary* between the competent department of the Holy See and each episcopal conference, a collaboration which must be *at the same time vigilant and creative.* We must keep our sights fixed on the greatness of the most holy Mystery and at the same time on spiritual movements and social changes, which are so significant for our times, since they not only sometimes create difficulties but also prepare us for a new way of participating in that great Mystery of Faith.

Above all I wish to emphasize that the problems of the liturgy, and in particular of the Eucharistic Liturgy, must not be *an occasion for dividing Catholics and for threatening the unity of the Church.* This is demanded by an elementary understanding of that sacrament which Christ has left us as the source of spiritual unity. And how could the Eucharist, which in the Church is the *sacramentum pietatis, signum unitatis, vinculum caritatis,*[72] form between us at this time a point of division and a source of distortion of thought and of behavior, instead of being the focal point and constitutive center, which it truly is in its essence, of the unity of the Church herself?

We are all equally indebted to our Redeemer. We should all listen together to that Spirit of truth and of love whom He has promised to the Church and who is operative in her. In the name of this truth and of this love, in the name of the crucified Christ and of His Mother, I ask you, and beg you: Let us abandon all opposition and division, and let us all unite in this great mission of salvation which is the price and at the same time the fruit of our redemption. The Apostolic See will continue to do all that is possible to provide the means of ensuring that unity of which we speak. Let everyone avoid anything in his own way of acting which could "grieve the Holy Spirit."[73]

In order that this unity and the constant and systematic collaboration which leads to it may be perseveringly continued, I beg on my knees that, through the intercession of Mary, holy spouse of the Holy Spirit and Mother of the Church, we may all receive the light of the Holy Spirit. And blessing everyone, with all my heart I once more address myself to you, my venerable and dear brothers in the episcopate, with a fraternal greeting and with full trust. In this collegial unity in which we share, let us do all we can to ensure that the Eucharist may become an ever greater source of life and light for the consciences of all our brothers and sisters of all the communities in the universal unity of Christ's Church on earth.

In a spirit of fraternal charity, to you and to all our confreres in the priesthood I cordially impart the apostolic blessing.

From the Vatican, February 24. First Sunday of Lent, in the year 1980, the second of the Pontificate.

Pope John Paul II

FOOTNOTES

1. Cf. Chapter 2: *AAS* 71 (1979), pp. 395f.
2. Cf. Ecumenical Council of Trent, Session XXII, Can. 2: *Conciliorum Oecumenicorum Decreta*, ed. 3, Bologna 1973, p. 735.

3. Because of this precept of the Lord, an Ethiopian Eucharistic Liturgy recalls that the Apostles "established for us patriarchs, archbishops, priests and deacons to celebrate the ritual of your holy Church": *Anaphora Sancti Athanasii: Prex Eucharistica*, Haenggi-Pahl, Fribourg (Switzerland) 1968, p. 183.

4. Cf. *La Tradition apostolique de saint Hippolyte*, nos. 2-4, ed. Botte, Münster-Westfalen 1963, pp. 5-17.

5. 2 Cor. 11:28.

6. 1 Pt. 2:5.

7. Cf. Second Vatican Ecumenical Council, Dogmatic Constitution on the Church, *Lumen gentium*, no. 28; *AAS* 57 (1965), pp. 33f.; Decree on the Ministry and Life of Priests, *Presbyterorum ordinis*, nos. 2, 5: *AAS* 58 (1966), pp. 993, 998; Decree on the Missionary Activity of the Church, *Ad gentes*, no. 39: *AAS* 58 (1966), p. 986.

8. Second Vatican Ecumenical Council, Dogmatic Constitution on the Church, *Lumen gentium*, no. 11: *AAS* 57 (1965), p. 15.

9. Jn. 3:16. It is interesting to note how these words are taken up by the liturgy of St. John Chrysostom immediately before the words of consecration and introduce the latter: cf. *La divina Liturgia del nostro Padre Giovanni Crisostomo*, Roma-Grottaferrata 1967, pp. 104f.

10. Cf. Mt. 26:26-28; Mk. 14:22-25; Lk. 22:18-20; 1 Cor. 11:23-25; cf. also the Eucharistic Prayers.

11. Phil. 2:8.

12. Jn. 13:1.

13. Cf. John Paul II, Homily in Phoenix Park, Dublin 7: *AAS* 71 (1979), pp. 1074ff.; Sacred Congregation of Rites, instruction *Eucharisticum Mysterium: AAS* 59 (1967), pp. 539-573; *Rituale Romanum, De sacra communione et de cultu Mysterii eucharistici extra Missam*, ed. typica, 1973. It should be noted that the value of the worship and the sanctifying power of these forms of devotion to the Eucharist depend not so much upon the forms themselves as upon interior attitudes.

14. Cf. *Bull Transiturus de hoc mundo* (Aug. 11, 1264): *Aemilii Friedberg, Corpus Iuris Canonici*, Pars II. *Decretalium Collectiones*, Leipzig 1881, pp. 1174-1177; *Studi*

eucharistici, VII Centenario della Bolla *'"Transiturus,"* 1264-1964, Orvieto 1966, pp. 302-317.

15. Cf. Paul VI, encyclical letter *Mysterium Fidei: AAS* 57 (1965), pp. 753-774; Sacred Congregation of Rites, Instruction *Eucharisticum mysterium: AAS* 59 (1967), pp. 539-573; *Rituale Romanum, De sacra communione et de cultu Mysterii eucharistici extra Missam, ed. typica,* 1973.

16. John Paul II, encyclical letter *Redemptor hominis,* no. 20: *AAS* 71 (1979), p. 311; cf. Second Vatican Ecumenical Council, Dogmatic Constitution on the Church, *Lumen gentium,* no. 11: *AAS* 57 (1965), pp. 15f.; also, note 57 to Schema II of the same dogmatic constitution, in *Acta Synodalia Sacrosancti Concilii Oecumenici Vaticani II,* vol. II, periodus 2a, pars I, public session II, pp. 251f.; Paul VI, address at the general audience of September 15, 1965: *Insegnamenti di Paolo VI,* III (1965), p. 103; H. de Lubac, *Méditation sur l'Eglise,* 2 ed., Paris 1963, pp. 129-137.

17. 1 Cor. 11:26.

18. Cf. Second Vatican Ecumenical Council, Dogmatic Constitution on the Church, *Lumen gentium,* no. 11: *AAS* 57 (1965) pp. 15f.; Constitution on the Sacred Liturgy, *Sacrosanctum concilium,* no. 10: *AAS* 56 (1964), p. 102; Decree on the Ministry and Life of Priests, *Presbyterorum ordinis,* no. 5: *AAS* 58 (1966), pp. 997f.; Decree on the Bishops' Pastoral Office in the Church, *Christus Dominus,* no. 30: *AAS* 58 (1966), pp. 688f.; Decree on the Church's Missionary Activity, *Ad gentes,* no. 9: *AAS* 58 (1966), pp. 957f.

19. Cf. Second Vatican Ecumenical Council, Dogmatic Constitution on the Church, *Lumen gentium,* no. 26: *AAS* 57 (1965), pp. 31f.; Decree on Ecumenism, *Unitatis redintegratio,* no. 15: *AAS* 57 (1965), pp. 101f.

20. This is what the Opening Prayer of Holy Thursday asks for: "We pray that in this Eucharist we may find the fullness of love and life": *Missale Romanum, ed. typica altera* 1975, p. 244; also the communion epiclesis of the Roman Missal: "May all of us who share in the body and blood of Christ be brought together in unity by the Holy Spirit. Lord, remember your Church throughout the world; make us grow in love": Eucharistic Prayer II: *ibid.,* pp. 458f.; Eucharistic Prayer III, p. 463.

21. Jn. 5:17.

22. Cf. Prayer after communion of the Mass for the Twenty-second Sunday in Ordinary Time: "Lord, you renew us at your table with the bread of life. May this food strengthen us in love and help us to serve you in each other": *Missale Romanum, ed. cit.*, p. 361.

23. Jn. 4:23.

24. Cf. 1 Cor. 10:17; commented upon by St. Augustine: *In Evangelium Ioannis* tract. 31, 13; *PL* 35, 1613; also commented upon by the Ecumenical Council of Trent, Session XIII, can. 8; *Conciliorum Oecumenicorum Decreta*, ed. 3, Bologna 1973, p. 697, 7; cf. Second Vatican Ecumenical Council, Dogmatic Constitution on the Church, *Lumen gentium*, no. 7: *AAS* 57 (1965), p. 9.

25. Jn. 13:35.

26. This is expressed by many prayers of the *Roman Missal:* the Prayer over the Gifts from the Common, "For those who work for the underprivileged"; "May we who celebrate the love of your Son also follow the example of your saints and grow in love for you and for one another": *Missale Romanum, ed. cit.*, p. 721; also the Prayer after Communion of the Mass "For Teachers": "May this holy meal help us to follow the example of your saints by showing in our lives the light of truth and love for our brothers": *ibid.*, p. 723; cf. also the Prayer after Communion of the Mass for the Twenty-second Sunday in Ordinary Time, quoted in note 22.

27. Jn. 4:23.

28. Eph. 4:13.

29. Cf. above, no. 2.

30. Cf. Second Vatican Ecumenical Council, Decree on the Missionary Activity of the Church, *Ad gentes*, nos. 9, 12: *AAS* 58 (1966), pp. 958-961f.; Decree on the Ministry and Life of Priests, *Presbyterorum ordinis*, no. 5: *AAS* 58 (1966), p. 997.

31. 1 Jn. 3:1.

32. Second Vatican Ecumenical Council, Dogmatic Constitution on the Church, *Lumen gentium*, no. 11: *AAS* 57 (1965), p. 15.

33. Cf. no. 20: *AAS* 71 (1979), pp. 313f.

34. 2 Pt. 3:13.

35. Col. 3:10.
36. Lk. 1:34; Jn. 6:69; Acts 3:14; Rv. 3:7.
37. Acts 10:38; Lk. 4:18.
38. Jn. 10:36.
39. Cf. Jn. 10:17.
40. Heb. 3:1; 4:15, etc.

41. As was stated in the ninth-century Byzantine liturgy, according to the most ancient codex, known formerly as *Barberino di San Marco* (Florence), and, now that it is kept in the Vatican Apostolic Library, as *Barberini Greco* 366f. 8 verso, lines 17-20. This part has been published by F. E. Brightman, *Liturgies Eastern and Western*, I. *Eastern Liturgies*, Oxford 1896, p. 318, 34-35.

42. Opening Prayer of the Second Votive Mass of the Holy Eucharist: *Missale Romanum, ed. cit.*, p. 858.

43. 1 Jn. 2:2; cf. *ibid.*, 4:10.

44. We speak of the *divinum Mysterium*, the *Sanctissimum*, the *Sacrosanctum*, meaning what is *sacred* and *holy* par excellence. For their part, the Eastern Churches call the Mass *raza* or *mysterion, hagiasmos, quddasa, qedasse*, that is to say "consecration" par excellence. Furthermore there are the liturgical rites, which, in order to inspire a sense of the sacred, prescribe silence, and standing or kneeling, and likewise professions of faith, and the incensation of the Gospel book, the altar, the celebrant and the sacred species. They even recall the assistance of the angelic beings created to serve the Holy God, i.e., with the *Sanctus* of our Latin Churches and the *Trisagion* and *Sancta Sanctis* of the Eastern liturgies.

45. For instance, in the invitation to receive Communion, this faith has been so formed as to reveal complementary aspects of the presence of Christ the Holy One: the epiphanic aspect noted by the Byzantines ("Blessed is he who comes in the name of the Lord: The Lord is God and *has appeared to us*": *La divina Liturgia del santo nostro Padre Giovanni Crisostomo*, Roma-Grottaferrata 1967, pp. 136f.); the aspect of relation and union sung of by the Armenians [Liturgy of St. Ignatius of Antioch: *"Unus Pater sanctus nobiscum, unus Filius sanctus nobiscum, unus Spiritus sanctus nobiscum"*: *Die Anaphora des heiligen Ignatius von*

Antiochien, übersetzt von A. Rücker, Oriens Christianus, 3ª ser., 5 [1930], p. 76); and the hidden heavenly aspect celebrated by the Chaldeans and Malabars (cf. the antiphonal hymn sung by the priest and the assembly after Communion: F. E. Brightman, *op. cit.*, p. 299.

46. Cf. Second Vatican Ecumenical Council, Constitution on the Sacred Liturgy, *Sacrosanctum concilium*, nos. 2, 47: *AAS* 56 (1964), pp. 83f.; 113; Dogmatic Constitution on the Church, *Lumen gentium*, nos. 3, 28: *AAS* 57 (1965), pp. 6, 33f.; Decree on Ecumenism, *Unitatis redintegratio*, no. 2: *AAS* 57 (1965), p. 91; Decree on the Ministry and Life of Priests, *Presbyterorum ordinis*, no. 13: *AAS* 58 (1966), pp. 1011f., Ecumenical Council of Trent, Session XXII, chap. I and II: *Conciliorum Oecumenicorum Decreta*, ed. 3, Bologna 1973, pp. 732f. especially: *una eademque est hostia, idem nunc offerens sacerdotum ministerio, qui se ipsum tunc in cruce obtulit, sola offerendi ratione diversa (ibid., p. 733).*

47. *Synodus Constantinopolita adversus Sotericum* (January 1156 and May 1157): Angelo Mai, *Spicilegium romanum*, t. X, Rome 1844, p. 77; *PG* 140, 190; cf. Martin Jugie, Dict. Theol. Cath., t. X, 1338; *Theologia dogmatica christianorum orientalium*, Paris, 1930, pp. 317-320.

48. *Instituto Generalis Missalis Romani*, 49c: *Missale Romanum, ed. cit.*, p. 39; cf. Second Vatican Ecumenical Council, Decree on the Ministry and Life of Priests *Presbyterorum ordinis*, 5: *AAS* 58 (1966), pp. 997f.

49. *Ordo Missae cum populo*, 18: *Missale Romanum, ed. cit.*, p. 390.

50. Cf. Ecumenical Council of Trent, Session 22, chap I, *Conciliorum Oecumenicorum Decreta*, ed. 3, Bologna 1973, pp. 732f.

51. Col. 2:14.

52. Jn. 11:28.

53. *Instituto Generalis Missalis Romani*, 55f.: *Missale Romanum, ed. cit.*, p. 40.

54. Cf. Constitution on the Sacred Liturgy *Sacrosanctum concilium*, nos. 35, 51: *AAS* 56 (1964), pp. 109, 114.

55. Cf. Sacred Congregation of Rites, Instruction *In edicendis normis*, VI, 17-18; VII, 19-20: *AAS* 57 (1965),

pp. 1012f.; Instruction *Musicam sacram*, IV, 48: *AAS* 59 (1967), p. 314; Decree, *De Titulo Basilicae Minoris*, II, 8: *AAS* 60 (1968), p. 538; Sacred Congregation for Divine Worship, Notif. *De Missali Romano, Liturgia Horarum et Calendario*, I, 4: *AAS* 63 (1971), p. 714.

56. Cf. Paul VI, Apostolic Constitution *Missale Romanum:* "We are fully confident that both priests and faithful will prepare their minds and hearts more devoutly for the Lord's Supper, meditating on the scriptures, nourished day by day with the words of the Lord": *AAS* 61 (1969), pp. 220f.; *Missale Romanum, ed. cit.*, p. 15.

57. Cf. *Pontificale romanum. De Institutione Lectorum et Acolythorum*, 4, *ed. typica*, 1972, pp. 19f.

58. Cf. *Instituto Generalis Missalis Romani*, 319-320: *Missale Romanum, ed. cit.*, p. 87.

59. Cf. Fr. J. Dolger, *Das Segnen der Sinne mit der Eucharistie. Eine altchristliche Kommunionsitte: Antike und Christentum*, t. 3 (1932), pp. 231-244; *Das Kultvergehen der Donatistin Lucilla von Karthago. Reliquienkuss vor dem Kuss der Eucharistie, ibid.*, pp. 245-252.

60. Cf. Second Vatican Ecumenical Council, Dogmatic Constitution on the Church, *Lumen gentium*, nos. 12, 35; *AAS* 57 (1965), pp. 16, 40.

61. Cf. Jn. 1:29; Rv. 19:9.

62. Cf. Lk. 14:16ff.

63. Cf. *Instituto Generalis Missalis Romani*, 7-8: *Missale Romanum, ed. cit.*, p. 29.

64. 1 Cor. 11:28.

65. *Pontificale Romanum. De Ordinatione Diaconi, Presbyteri et Episcopi, ed. typica*, 1968, p. 93.

66. Heb. 5:1.

67. Sacred Congregation of Rites, Instruction *Eucharisticum Mysterium: AAS* 59 (1967), pp. 539-573; *Rituale Romanum. De sacra communione et de cultu Mysterii eucharistici extra Missam, ed. typica*, 1973; Sacred Congregation for Divine Worship, *Litterae circulares ad Conferentiarum Episcopalium Praesides de precibus eucharisticis: AAS* 65 (1973), pp. 340-347.

68. Nos. 38-63: *AAS* 59 (1967), pp. 586-592.

69. *AAS* 64 (1972), pp. 518-525. Cf. also the *Com-*

municatio published the following year for the correct application of the above-mentioned Instruction: *AAS* 65 (1973), pp. 616-619.

70. Cf. Second Vatican Ecumenical Council, Dogmatic Constitution on the Church, *Lumen gentium*, 12: *AAS* 57 (1965), pp. 16f.

71. Mt. 13:52.

72. Cf. St. Augustine, *In Evangelium Ioannis tract.* 26, 13: *PL* 35, 1612f.

73. Eph. 4:30.

Generously Available for the Church's Needs

On June 1, 1980, after his address to the French bishops, the Holy Father went to the auditorium of the seminary at Issy les Moulineaux where he met the 220 seminarians and numerous members of the priests' councils of the Paris region. He spoke to them as follows.

Dear seminarian friends,

1. I could not conclude this afternoon without spending a moment with you, getting to know your faces, and exhorting you in the name of the Lord. What joy to meet you, you young students in formation in the Paris region! I have been told that there are gathered here the students of the St. Sulpice Seminary, those of the University Seminary of the Carmelites and members of different preparatory groups. Fine. I am happy that it is possible to count on your availability to serve, on your generosity. Addressing these few words to you, you will allow me to address at the same time all your French confreres who, elsewhere in this country, but also in my diocese of Rome, are following the same way.

As you know, I have just had a long working-session with your bishops. It was a particularly important conversation, in the course of which we were able, we who are jointly in charge of all the Churches, to face up to our responsibilities in order to assume them according to what pleases God. And now, it seems quite natural to continue this conversation, in a way, with those who are preparing to become collaborators of the episcopal order, and to be associated in this way, in the Person of Christ, with the preaching of the Gospel and the guidance of the People of God. You are still young, certainly, but already you divine a great many things. You understand that your gift must be complete and that, the further you go, the more you will discover the necessity of making it—if I may venture to say so—even more complete. It is at this level, therefore, that I will take up my position with you, taking into account, of course, the fact that a way such as yours takes time, and a long spiritual, intellectual and pastoral maturation, and that the mere desire to become a priest is not enough in itself to meet the requirements of the priesthood.

Discover the Sense of Self-Sacrifice

2. One of these requirements, the most fundamental one, is that you should be deeply rooted in Jesus Christ. I invite you to this with all my heart. If you could learn, through prayer and contemplation, to live, preach, love and suffer like Christ, it seems that the main lines of your mission would gradually take shape clearly, and that you would also feel a vital need to join men and bring them what they really need. In such a

proceeding there is already the soul of the apostolate, so that "action" is indissolubly linked with "being," and vice versa. Here it is not useful to pursue vain discussions, nor is it good to prefer one to the detriment of the other. The Church intends to form you in complete interior unity, in which the mission requires intimacy with God, and in which the latter calls for the former.

Do you not want to be, yourselves, "good shepherds"? The good shepherd gives his life, and he gives his life for his sheep. Very well, then! It is necessary to discover the sense of self-sacrifice, linked with the sacrifice of Christ, and offer yourselves for others, who expect this witness from you. That can be said of all the faithful, but with all the more reason and in a very special way of priests and future priests. May your daily participation in the Eucharist and the efforts you make to increase Eucharistic devotion within you, help you along this way!

Pastoral Wisdom

3. I was speaking to you a moment ago of unity among yourselves. In my opinion, it makes it possible to acquire what could be called pastoral wisdom. One of the fruits of the conciliar decree of Vatican II on the formation of priests was certainly to create the conditions for better pastoral preparation of candidates. Thanks to the inner balance you achieve, you must be able to improve your judgment of men, things and situations, and view them in the light of God and not with the eyes of the world. That will lead you

to a deep perception of the problems, and of the multiple urgent needs of the mission, and at the same time that will urge you on towards the right goal. In this way you will be less exposed to the temptation of "extolling" only what our contemporaries are living, or on the contrary of experimenting on them pastoral ideas that are perhaps generous, but personal and without the guarantee of the Church: there must be no experimenting on men. You will take to heart, for this very reason, your intellectual work, indispensable today as it is after ordination, in order to transmit to others the whole content of faith in an exact, harmonious synthesis, easy to assimilate.

Is it necessary, besides, to point out that the priest is one among others? By himself, he cannot be everything to everyone. His ministry is exercised within a presbyterium, around a bishop. Such already in a small way is your own case, to the extent that your bonds with your diocese, where you are integrated in the pastoral teams to develop in you the capacity of working as a Church, are gradually strengthened. And if your personal path—or the stress sometimes laid on such and such an aspect of your preparation —make you more suitable for a given type of ministry, among a more particular category of the population, nevertheless you will be sent basically to everyone, with pastoral concern for everyone and the determination to collaborate with everyone, excluding no trend or environment. You must be capable also of accepting any ministry that is entrusted to you, without subordinating your acceptance to conformity with expediency or personal projects. In this matter, it is the needs of the Church that have priority, and it is necessary to adapt oneself to them. This seems absolutely essential to your bishops and myself, in consideration of the office with which Providence has invested us and with which you will be associated one day.

With Faith and Joy

4. My dear sons, you see the vastness of the task, the vastness of the needs. You are not very numerous, and yet the efforts undertaken for several years are beginning to yield visible results. I shall not tell you that the generosity of the laity will make it possible to mitigate the lack of priests. It is completely of another order. In the laity you will always have to develop the sense of responsibility and to educate them to take their full place in the community. But what God has put in your hearts through His call corresponds to a specific vocation. Try to bear witness better to your faith and your joy. You are the witnesses of priestly vocations among adolescents and young people of your age. Ah! If you could realize the hope that is in you, and show that the mission cannot wait, in France and even more in other less privileged countries! I encourage you with all my strength to be the first apostles of vocations.

Priests of Quality

5. I also wish to encourage and thank your teachers and educators at all levels: rectors of

seminaries, diocesan delegates, parish priests, chaplaincies and movements which contribute to your formation, and those who enabled you to discern the Lord's call. You owe them a great deal. The Church owes them a great deal. In this place, I would like to pay tribute especially to priests of the Society of St. Sulpice, who have won the esteem of everyone in their service of the priesthood.

Your educators have a difficult task. It must be known, in France, that I put my trust in them and give them my brotherly support. They wish to form priests of quality. May they continue their efforts and develop them further, with the help of the texts of the Council, the excellent *Rationes* which have been prepared at the request of the Holy See, and the recent documents published by the Congregation for Catholic Education, which they have, I do not doubt, distributed widely among you and commented upon.

My hearty thanks to you all, dear confreres and dear sons. I shall see you later, at the *Parc des Princes*, with the young people of the Paris region, and I bless you with my deep affection.

Meet the New Realities of Seminaries Responsibly

On January 5, 1982, the Holy Father received in audience the rectors, spiritual directors and prefects of studies of all the ninety-two major seminaries of Italy, who had arrived in Rome for a meeting organized by the Episcopal Commission for Catholic Education of the Italian Episcopal Conference (CEI). The subject of the meeting was "Unity in formation for the priesthood." The group was led by Cardinal Anastasio Ballestrero, President of the Italian Episcopal Conference; Bishop Antonio Ambrosanio, President of the CEI's Episcopal Commission for Catholic Education, and other bishops on the Commission or otherwise involved in seminaries.

John Paul II delivered the following address.

Venerated brothers in the episcopate,
Beloved sons,

1. Addressing to you my cordial greeting, I wish to express the deep joy I experience in this meeting with you who are responsible for the priestly formation imparted in the major seminaries of Italy.

You have gathered in Rome, at the invitation of the CEI's Episcopal Commission for Catholic Education, for a more careful and thorough reflection—particularly in the light of the national *Ratio Institutionis* on "The formation of priests in the Italian Church"—dedicated to a subject which has always been the object of the Holy See's solicitude, but which has recently become also a reason for concern. It is a question of the problem, an old and still relevant one, of ensuring the Church the ministers that she needs.

On the occasion of the opening of the Second International Congress for Vocations, held in Rome in May of last year, I was offered the opportunity of again confirming clearly that the problem of priestly vocations is the fundamental problem of the Church. Priestly vocations are in fact the verification and expression of her vitality, and at the same time they are the condition of her mission and her development. And saying this I was thinking, as is obvious, particularly of the seminaries, whose purpose is to welcome and cultivate vocations.

Renewed Requirements

2. The very organization of this meeting, made possible by your qualified presence, is a significant testimony of the determination of the Italian Church to work in this very delicate area. And I warmly encourage you to meet better and better the renewed requirements of your delicate office. Your presence is, in fact, a consoling sign of the confidence you place in Him who is the first source of the priestly vocation.

I am happy, therefore, to express to the well-deserving promoters and organizers of the meeting, to all of you here present, rectors, spiritual directors, headmasters and prefects of studies, my hearty thanks and sincere satisfaction. And, in you, I wish to thank and encourage also those who share with you—at the various levels—the heavy task of preparing future priests.

Common awareness of the difficult situation—clearly indicated by the statistics—in which many centers of ecclesiastical formation in Italy find themselves today, although consoling signs of revival are not lacking, prompts some reflections which directly concern the life and progress of seminaries in your country.

You know very well that the Church does not intend either to conceal the problems that are posed for seminaries today, or to remain extraneous to the way in which these problems are met and solved. It is the Second Vatican Council itself which commits us to reflection and research in this area. But it is also the Council which offers us the criteria and guidelines concerning particularly the spiritual, disciplinary and intellectual preparation of candidates for the priesthood.

Spiritual Preparation

3. Spiritual preparation, in the first place. The educational effort of the seminary must aim at bringing the youth to the knowledge and personal experience of the Lord, in order to mold in him a pastor of souls, who, in his person and in his activity, will appear and really be "a servant of Christ and a steward of the mysteries of God" (cf. 1 Cor. 4:1).

Among the aspects that seem to deserve particular consideration in the spiritual preparation of future priests, I would like to submit to your attention those so opportunely indicated in the circular letter of the Sacred Congregation for Catholic Education on "Some more urgent aspects of spiritual formation in the seminaries" (Jan. 6, 1980). They can be summed up in the following points:

a) to train priests who will accept and deeply love Christ, the Word of God, our Brother, Friend and Savior;

b) to train priests who can see in the Paschal Mystery the supreme expression of the love that the Word had for us, sacrificing Himself for the Church—*in finem dilexit eos;*

c) to train priests who are not afraid to recognize that real communion and concrete friendship with Christ entail an asceticism, and therefore a commitment to renunciation and sacrifice;

d) to make the seminary a school of filial love for her who is the Mother of Jesus and our mother.

In this field the work of the spiritual director, who has the task of contributing to the formation of truly priestly men, is still determinant and irreplaceable. His action is to be considered fundamental in educational work, since it constitutes a decisive moment to create in the student's heart that image of Christ to which he will have to refer as his supreme ideal throughout his life. To be such, spiritual direction must take the shape of a serious relationship, clear, open,

Intellectual Growth

5. Finally, there is intellectual preparation. Application to study—an effective means of growth and personal improvement—is, together with piety, the great daily duty of the seminarian, his professional work. For students of the philosophical and theological courses, study takes on a particularly full and profound dimension, because it must now serve as an aid and enrichment of the life of faith and as an indispensable instrument for the future ministry. It is necessary in particular that knowledge of the movements of philosophical thought and of literature, the reading of the events of history and of the cultural and social formation of peoples, and the whole humanistic formation in general should give the future pastor of souls that capacity of interpreting the outstanding stages of human civilization in a Christian key, in order to be truly a spiritual guide for his contemporaries, especially for youth. On this basis there must be inserted the study of theology, in all its branches, which opens to the seminarian a complete view of the divine plan of salvation, and offers him the irreplaceable instruments of his ministerial and catechetical activity, at which he is aiming with all his strength.

The growing importance attributed to study in the preparation of future priests is happily testified to by the creation in your country, in the last few years, of theological institutes or centers affiliated to a theology faculty. This in fact serves to raise the level of philosophical and theological studies, to offer the possibility of obtaining the bachelor's degree, and to encourage closer and more advantageous collaboration between the diocesan clergy and the religious clergy. I wish moreover to point out with satisfaction that the above-mentioned institutes are also assuming the precious function of centers to promote the cultural *aggiornamento* of priests, in the important initiative of "ongoing formation" which must be sustained and promoted with every effort.

In this framework stress must be laid on the figure of the headmaster or prefect of studies, who especially has the duty to achieve unity of teaching, coordinating the individual disciplines; to see that a complete teaching of the doctrine of the Church is offered, in an eminently pastoral view, according to the directions of Vatican II; to drive home to students that what they learn in the seminary does not exhaust their commitment of study, but must rather stimulate in them the desire for continual updating, as the Council likewise asked. And everything, needless to say, must be carried out in an atmosphere of faithful adherence to the Magisterium of the Church, testified also by the discernment with which students are directed towards authors who, in their works, show that they draw inspiration from it loyally.

Eagerness for Truth and Certainties

Beloved in Christ,

From the testimonies that come to me from various quarters, I know that the students in our seminaries—after a period of adjustment, consideration and reflection—are more desirous today of meditation, and are seeking with great commitment to study more deeply the essential values of faith and prayer. They show that they are more eager for truth and certainties, and manifest the clear need for binding and total choices.

It is up to you, rectors, spiritual directors and teachers, to carry out the difficult and indispensable task of responding to the new realities that have been created in our seminaries: with adequate pedagogical, didactic and cultural preparation; with an educational commitment which will encourage personal relations of dialogue, research and verification among all those responsible for formation, and with the students; with wide opening to the problems of society; with close collaboration of the seminary with the diocesan presbyterate.

I am certain you will not miss such an eagerly-awaited appointment, which cannot be delayed. I place my confidence in your ability, your will and your sense of responsibility.

With these sentiments I willingly impart my apostolic blessing to you, to your collaborators and to all your seminarians, and I beg you to convey to them the expression of my affection and the assurance of my constant remembrance in prayer.

"Do Whatever He Tells You!"

On January 30, 1982, Pope John Paul paid a visit to the Pontifical Philippine College in Rome. During the Mass celebrated in the college chapel, the Holy Father delivered the following homily.

Your Eminences, my brother bishops, dearly beloved,

My message today is above all directed to the priests who make up the student body of this Philippine College here in Rome. It is especially for you, my brother priests, that I have come. At the same time I am thinking of all the Filipino people, with cherished memories of my visit to your country, memories which, in union with Christ, I offer to the Father in this Eucharistic Sacrifice.

1. This afternoon Jesus is gathering us together as His disciples. We are celebrating our union with Him. We are celebrating Christ's union with His Church, a covenant of love that is signified in the sacrament of marriage. And like the marriage feast of Cana our own celebration today is complete: in discipleship we have assembled with Jesus to be strengthened by His company, to enter more deeply into His friendship and to share His Paschal Supper. At the

same time we know that the Mother of Jesus is here. We feel at peace; we feel secure for the journey that awaits us in life. For we are gathered under the patronage of Mary, *Nuestra Señora de la Paz y Buen Viaje,* to whom this college is dedicated.

The Purpose of College

2. Today's event evokes the whole reality of the religious history of the Filipino people. Young men are sent by their bishops to this college so that they may be prepared to enter into a centuries-old tradition of fidelity and evangelization. Here young men come in order to be enlisted and equipped in the cause of the Gospel. As John XXIII pointed out at the time that this college was inaugurated, the very institution is also a special link between the Philippines and the See of Peter.

Here, by the grace of God, the ideals of the priesthood are to be lived by individual priests who are supported by a community which corporately embraces and promotes the same ideals. From here these ideals are to be transmitted to seminaries and parishes throughout the Philippines. Here young priests can reflect deeply on what it means to be sent to proclaim the Gospel of salvation. What a great hope therefore is held out by this institution to the Filipino people; it represents their hope and prayer and plea to have priests according to the heart of Jesus Christ.

In my talk to the priests and seminarians in Cebu, I said how much the Church needs her priests. And today I would add how much the Philippine College can do to help priests to fulfill their mission and thus meet the needs of the Church. Here you have the opportunity to form, through the Eucharist, a true community which expresses itself in prayer, charity and zeal. As you prepare to become ministers of reconciliation for the People of God, authentic heralds of deep interior conversion, you have the wonderful opportunity to learn, through personal use, to love the Sacrament of Penance and to give it the very high priority that it is meant to have in the Church today. In your community you also have the opportunity to look to the future, reflecting, in the light of God's Word, on the ecclesial situation that awaits you in your respective dioceses. In prayer and meditation and through your dedicated study, the Lord will speak to you and inflame your hearts with zeal for the well being of the Filipino people. You will begin to realize more and more how urgent the cause of evangelization is, how much the Church needs you, how much Christ needs you—because He has willed to need you—in order to continue His salvific mission. But at the same time you will see that there are conditions for a truly effective priesthood, for a truly effective collaboration with Christ the High Priest.

The Need for Intimacy with Jesus Christ

3. In Cebu I spoke of three of these conditions. There is above all the need for intimacy

with Jesus Christ—the kind of intimate union to which Christ called His Apostles. They were His closest friends, the companions He chose personally, the ones with whom He shared His thoughts, and to whom He finally entrusted the mission which He had received from His Father. A second condition for an effective priesthood is the absolute need for unity with the bishop, in the fraternity of the presbyterium. Jesus wills that our visible unity in the priesthood should reflect the source of His own inner dynamism: His union with the Father. From earliest times the Fathers of the Church proclaimed this truth with eloquence and insistence. The third condition for a fruitful service to God's People is the total gift of our being to Christ. In giving ourselves entirely to Him—through the gift we make of our celibacy—we receive as a gift from Christ the power to love more deeply all those who make up the "whole Christ." In calling us to the priesthood, Jesus calls us to generous and sacrificial love.

Fidelity to Mary, Obedience to Jesus

4. By reason of our very baptism in Christ, we are called by the Father to holiness, as St. Paul reminds us in the reading this afternoon: "Before the world was made, he chose us, chose us in Christ, to be holy and spotless, and to live through love" (Eph. 1:4). These words take on new intensity for us here. To live as adopted sons means even more to us when we reflect that we are identified with Jesus, the only Son, in His

role as High Priest, constituted as such at the moment of His Incarnation in the womb of the Virgin Mary. Mary presides over the destiny of this college, just as she has presided for centuries over evangelization in the Philippines. She is close to all those who share the priesthood of her Son. In today's Gospel account she breaks the silence that generally surrounds her in order to give these words of counsel: "Do whatever he tells you" (Jn. 2:5). The Gospel relates how in fidelity to Mary's suggestion and in obedience to Christ's words there were undreamt of results. Jesus performed the "first sign" of His Gospel ministry.

Today Mary is still saying: "Do whatever he tells you." And through fidelity to her and in obedience to Jesus, we are sure that we shall continue to have results. We believe that Jesus will perform other "signs" of His power and love, to meet the needs of His Church, in spite of the inadequacies of His servants.

To Preach the Word

5. If we listen attentively, we know that Jesus is telling us to prepare for our mission of evangelization, so that we can go forth preaching a Gospel of salvation, announcing the Good News that is for all the people, proclaiming, in the very words of Jesus: "God so loved the world that he gave his only Son, that whoever believes in him should not perish but have eternal life. For God sent the Son into the world, not to condemn the world, but that the world might be saved through

him" (Jn. 3:16-17). If we listen to Mary and if we obey Jesus we know that our ministry of evangelization will be blessed. For this reason we are convinced that this is a day of hope for this college and for its students and staff. With God's help this institution will truly fulfill its providential role at the service of continuing evangelization throughout the Philippines. It is a day of hope for all Asia, with the light of Christ shining from the Philippines.

6. Dear brothers, always remember that the Mother of Jesus is here; she is with us today, and she will continue to be with you in your preparation for your future mission at home. She will accompany you on your journey of evangelization throughout your land. Act on her words: listen to Jesus as He invites you to great intimacy with Himself, union with your bishops and renewed dedication to generous and faithful celibate love in the service of evangelization. It will always be so. Wherever you are, you can say: the Mother of Jesus is here!

Also Available:
To the Church in America

How does the Church meet the needs of people in North America? In this volume, Pope John Paul II and his immediate Predecessors, Pope Paul VI and Pope John Paul I, answer the concerns of Bishops, Priests, Religious and Laity. Each in his own way calls us to:

- "A renewed commitment to God's Word"
- "a profound respect and esteem for ethical and religious values"
- "the worth of every human person"
- "the holiness of personal conversion"
- "the cause of Catholic education...the cause of Jesus Christ and of His Gospel at the service of man"
- "supporting and defending the family"
- "a new era of Eucharistic piety"
- "a profound respect for the laws of the Creator and Lord of life"
- "a more diligent and fruitful use of the Sacrament of Penance"
- "a renewal of love...a real civilization of love"
- "the undiluted message of the Gospel"
- "the true progress of ecumenism"
- "a deeper understanding of social responsibility"

The Vicars of Christ assure us: "We are close to our people in their problems and difficulties. They must always know that we love them."

166 pages; cloth $4.00; paper $3.00 — EP1065

Coming Soon!

A two-volume collection of the words of Pope John Paul II directed to Bishops and Priests throughout the world. Over 215 talks included: from the beginning of his pontificate, October, 1978—May, 1981. Each volume (approximately 700 pages) cloth $12.95; paper $11.95

The Dimensions of the Priesthood
Compiled by the Daughters of St. Paul

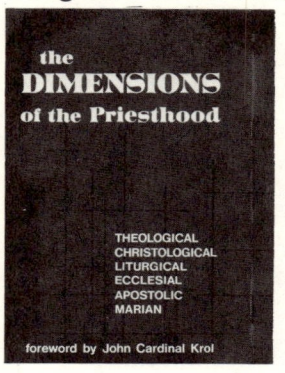

"An indispensable book in the library of every cleric ...a source book, a book of meditations, a book of prayer and of spiritual reading"—John Cardinal Krol. A timely compilation of 325 selected passages from the documents of Vatican II, from postconciliar documents, from the writings and addresses of Popes Pius XII, John XXIII, Paul VI and the World Synod of Bishops. 324 pages cloth $5.75; paper $4.50 — SP0110

Meditation Notes on Paul the Apostle, Model of the Spiritual Life
Rev. James Alberione, SSP, STD

These writings of Father James Alberione, Founder of the Pauline Family, were discovered after his death in November, 1971. They are meditation notes and resolutions made during a course of spiritual exercises. The theme is St. Paul and the priest. Every priest and spiritual guide can find in these pages a great wealth of material. 100 pages cloth $2.00 — SP0420

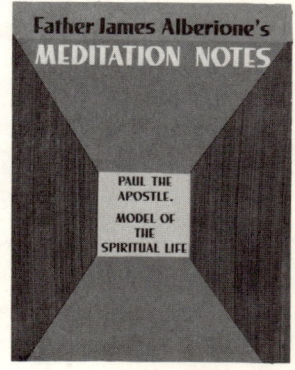

Daughters of St. Paul

IN MASSACHUSETTS
  50 St. Paul's Ave., Jamaica Plain, Boston, MA 02130;
    617-522-8911; 617-522-0875
  172 Tremont Street, Boston, MA 02111; **617-426-5464;
    617-426-4230**
IN NEW YORK
  78 Fort Place, Staten Island, NY 10301; **212-447-5071**
  59 East 43rd Street, New York, NY 10017; **212-986-7580**
  625 East 187th Street, Bronx, NY 10458; **212-584-0440**
  525 Main Street, Buffalo, NY 14203; **716-847-6044**
IN NEW JERSEY
  Hudson Mall — Route 440 and Communipaw Ave.,
    Jersey City, NJ 07304; **201-433-7740**
IN CONNECTICUT
  202 Fairfield Ave., Bridgeport, CT 06604; **203-335-9913**
IN OHIO
  2105 Ontario St. (at Prospect Ave.), Cleveland, OH 44115; **216-621-9427**
  25 E. Eighth Street, Cincinnati, OH 45202; **513-721-4838**
IN PENNSYLVANIA
  1719 Chestnut Street, Philadelphia, PA 19103; **215-568-2638**
IN VIRGINIA
  1025 King St., Alexandria, VA 22314 **703-683-1741**
IN FLORIDA
  2700 Biscayne Blvd., Miami, FL 33137; **305-573-1618**
IN LOUISIANA
  4403 Veterans Memorial Blvd., Metairie, LA 70002; **504-887-7631;
    504-887-0113**
  1800 South Acadian Thruway, P.O. Box 2028, Baton Rouge, LA 70821
    504-343-4057; 504-343-3814
IN MISSOURI
  1001 Pine Street (at North 10th), St. Louis, MO 63101; **314-621-0346;
    314-231-1034**
IN ILLINOIS
  172 North Michigan Ave., Chicago, IL 60601; **312-346-4228
    312-346-3240**
IN TEXAS
  114 Main Plaza, San Antonio, TX 78205; **512-224-8101**
IN CALIFORNIA
  1570 Fifth Avenue, San Diego, CA 92101; **714-232-1442**
  46 Geary Street, San Francisco, CA 94108; **415-781-5180**
IN HAWAII
  1143 Bishop Street, Honolulu, HI 96813; **808-521-2731**
IN ALASKA
  750 West 5th Avenue, Anchorage AK 99501; **907-272-8183**
IN CANADA
  3022 Dufferin Street, Toronto 395, Ontario, Canada
IN ENGLAND
  128, Notting Hill Gate, London W11 3QG, England
  133 Corporation Street, Birmingham B4 6PH, England
  5A-7 Royal Exchange Square, Glasgow G1 3AH, England
  82 Bold Street, Liverpool L1 4HR, England
IN AUSTRALIA
  58 Abbotsford Rd., Homebush, N.S.W., Sydney 2140, Australia